LEARN TO P

CRICKET

Script By : *T. R. Bhanot*

Artwork By : *Pushpa Verma*

Published by
DREAMLAND PUBLICATIONS
J-128, KIRTI NAGAR, NEW DELHI - 110 015 (INDIA)
Tel : 011-2510 6050 Fax : 011-2543 8283
E-mail : dreamland@vsnl.com
Shop online at www.dreamlandpublications.com
Like us on www.facebook.com/DreamlandPublications

Published in 2014 by :

DREAMLAND PUBLICATIONS

J-128, Kirti Nagar, New Delhi - 110 015 (India)

Phone : 011 - 2545 5657, 2510 6050, Fax : 011 - 2543 8283

ISBN 978-81-8451-709-5

INTRODUCTION

The game of cricket has a long history. It is a bat-and-ball team sport. It is believed that it was originally a children's game, but references indicate that during the 17th century, it became a well established sport played by adults. In the 18th century, cricket became the national sport of England.

Test cricket is the highest standard of first-class cricket. Test matches are played between two teams, each containing a group of eleven players. The matches are called series which last upto five-days and a series normally consists of three to five matches. With its great popularity, cricket entered a new era of limited Over Cricket or One-Day Matches. Each team in One-Day Cricket plays one innings only and faces a limited number of overs, a maximum of 50. The first Limited Overs International was played in 1971. The governing International Cricket Council (ICC) staged the first Cricket World Cup in 1975.

In the 21st century, a new limited overs form Twenty-20 has made an immediate impact. The concept of twenty-20 was introduced in England in 2003, to provide workers with an evening entertainment.

Though the game of cricket has a complex history, but with its greatest popularity, it is the world's second most popular sport with approx. 100 member countries.

— Publishers

The Major Cricket Playing Countries:—

The International Cricket Council (ICC) is the governing body for International Test Match. One Day International Cricket and Twenty-20 Internationals. The Full Members are automatically qualified to play all the forms of crickets. There are ten Full members of the International Cricket Council. West Indies cricket team does not represent one country, but rather an amalgamation of over 20 countries adn territories from the Caribbean. The English Cricket team represents both England and Wales. The teams and their logos are:

Australia

Bangladesh

England

India

New Zealand

International Cricket Council

Pakistan

South Africa

Sri Lanka

West Indies

Zimbabwe

Other Cricket Playing Countries and their logos :—

Ireland

Netherlands

Canada

Kenya

Afghanistan

CONTENTS

Chapter One

Starting Cricket

ABOUT THE GAME

Cricket is a game skies apart from most of the other sports. It is full of a variety of techniques and a lot of room for shrewdness and intrigue. It involves both brain and brawn—flexible athletic body bubbling with agility, instinctive action and brainy moves. All these qualities are needed as cricket has its set rules and procedures that can well make one's head spin dizzily.

The game of cricket is played using a bat and a ball by two teams—each with 11 players. Teams may consist of men or of women. Both the teams take turns to bat and to field. Each member of the batting side is called a batsman.

Batsmen come one by one to face the bowling action of the fielding side and try to score maximum possible runs in order to build up a challenging total. When ten of the batsmen

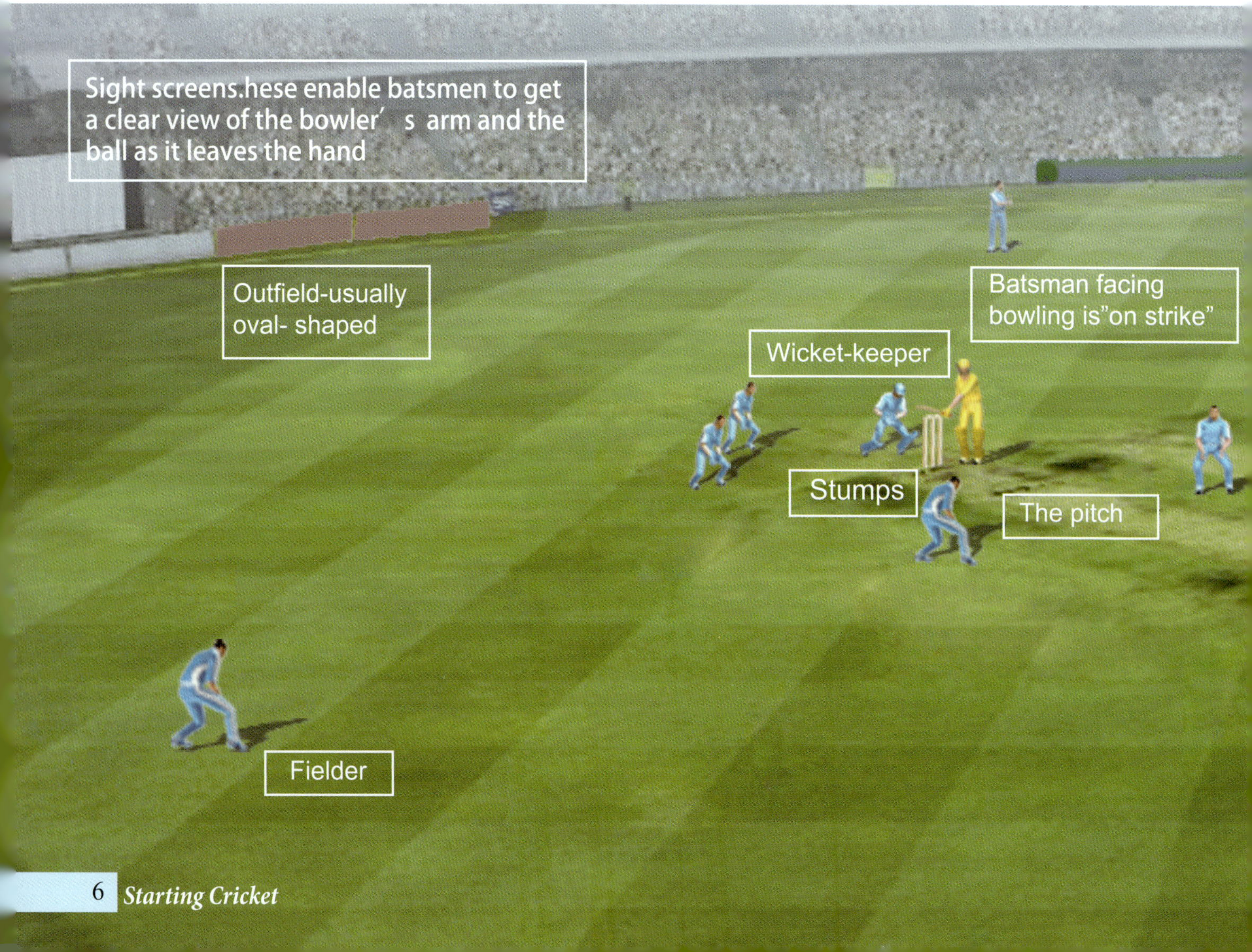

are out, the team's innings comes to an end and the other side goes in to bat. The earlier batting side has to take up fielding. The team that is able to score more runs during its batting session is the winner.

THE FIELD

A cricket field may be any shape though it is generally oval or round. Though other laws of the game are very exact, yet they are not specific about the field. But one thing that these laws insist on regarding the cricket field is that the boundary, i.e. the outer edge of the playing area must be marked very clearly. It aims at enabling the umpires to decide when four runs have been scored and when six runs have been scored. The boundary is generally marked using a clear-cut line or a rope. Remember that—

(a) Four runs are scored if the ball after the strike bounces on the outfield before reaching the boundary line.

(b) Six runs are scored if the ball after the strike goes beyond the boundary line without bouncing on the outfield.

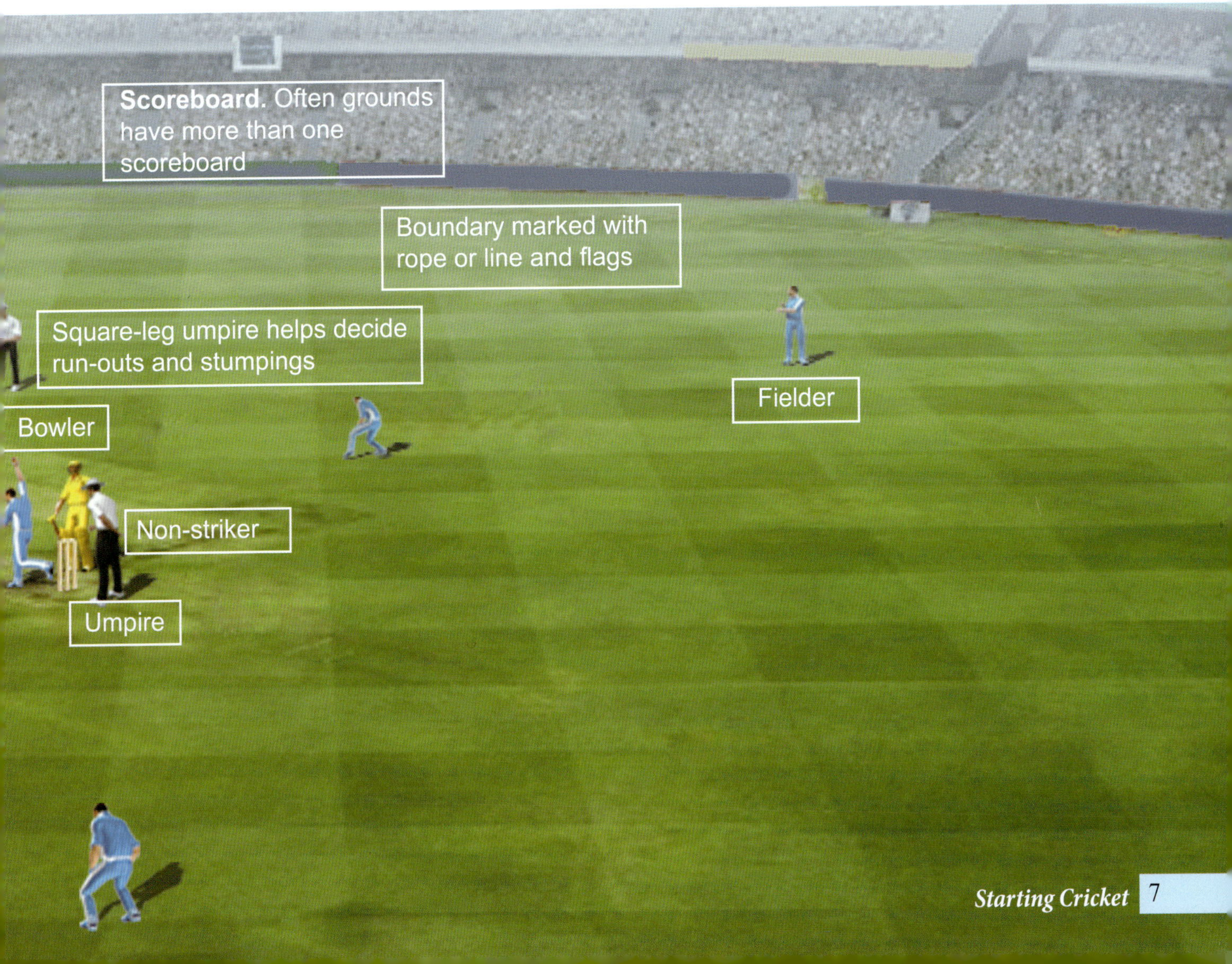

THE PITCH

The pitch covers the central part of the field in the form of an oblong belt which is 3 metres wide. On either side, it has a wicket consisting of three stumps capped by two bails. The wickets are 20.12 metres apart and stand parallel to each other. The area between the wickets is called the pitch, i.e. the real playing area. It is here that cricket matches are won or lost.

Each wicket is 22.9 centimtres wide with its stumps close enough not to allow the ball pass between any two of them. The stumps have their tops 71.1 centimetres above the ground. The bails are 11.1 centimetres long and rest in the grooves on top of the stumps not rising more than 13 millimetres above the stumps.

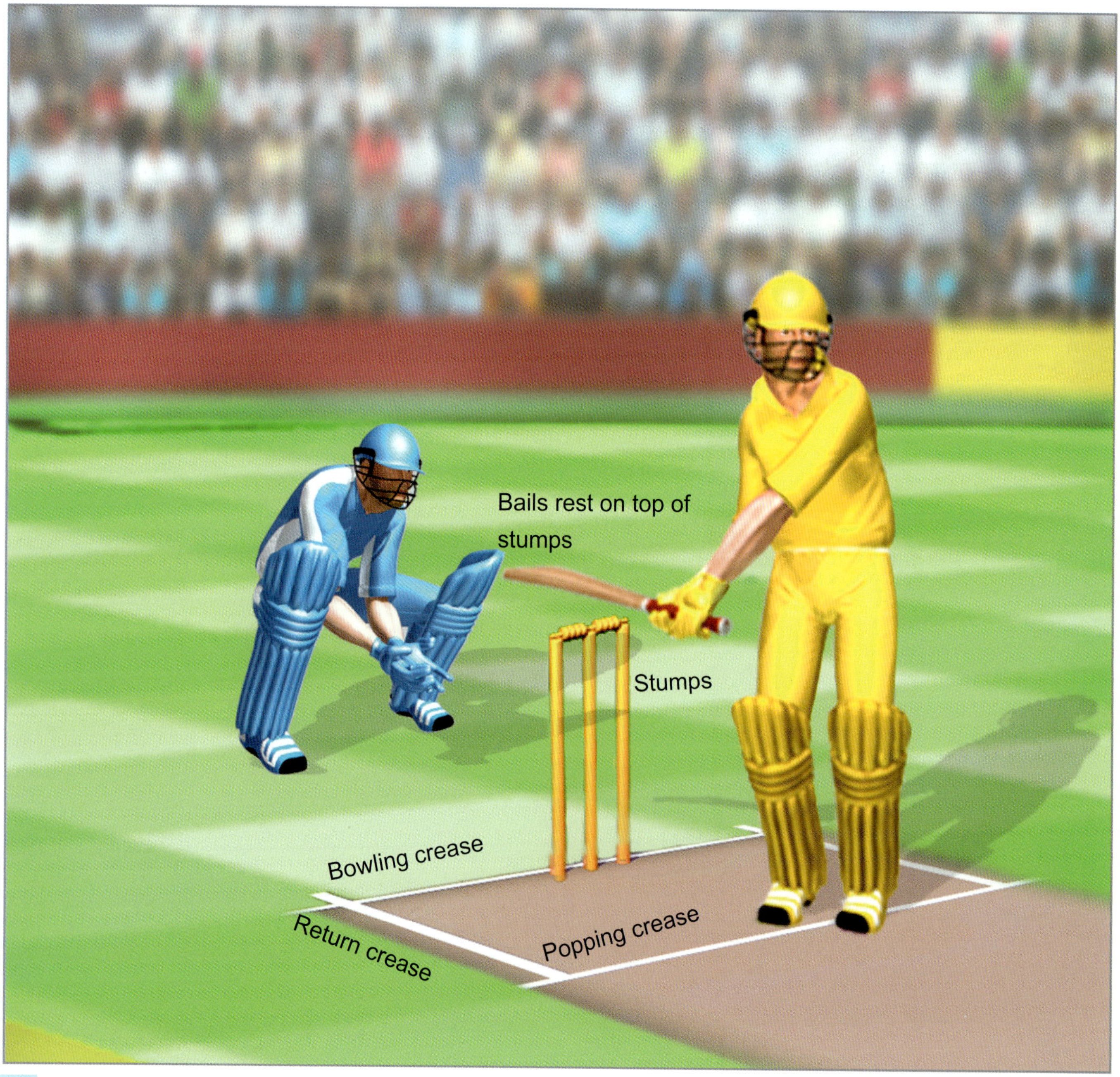

A PERFECT PITCH

A perfect pitch—is a misleading term indeed. A pitch consists of soil and grass. So pitches are natural, not artificial. But it is true that some careful steps can make a pitch more suitable for playing conditions. Equally true is the fact that like beauty, a pitch lies in the view of the player. If a pitch is perfect for a team or player, it can be terrible or disastrous for another.

THE ROLE OF THE PITCH

Still the role of the pitch is vital in a cricket game. That is why captains and other players examine the pitch before a game is to be played. Changes in teams can be made after examining a pitch. A pitch can be hard, fast or bouncy. Different kinds of pitch often help different types of bowlers. A pitch may cause the ball to turn also. A pitch is often damp because of dew in the morning and such a pitch helps seam bowlers.

A pitch is prepared by the ground staff. Even then a pitch may prove in favour of one side—either the batting side or the bowling side. But if a pitch proves dangerous for batting, a match may be abandoned. It was what happened in the Jamaica Test Match during England's tour of the West Indies in the year 1998.

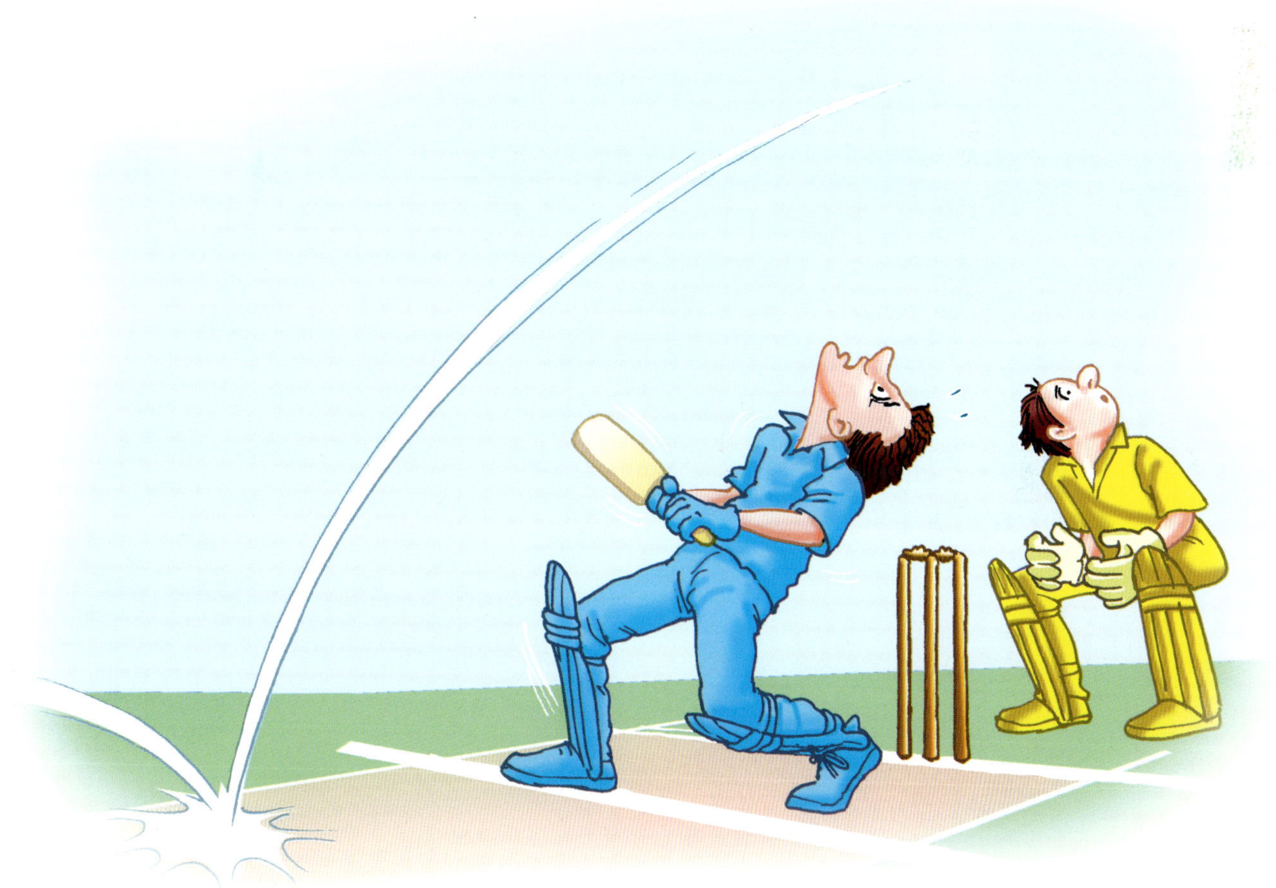

POSITIONS

Positions is a term in cricket in regard to the players of the fielding side, except the bowler and the wicket-keeper. The picture given below explains the name and location of each of the fielders. It is the captain who directs each fielder to his position considering the bowler and whether the striking batsman is right-handed or left-handed. These positions may be a bit confusing for a new cricketer. But once he/she has followed the basic positioning, all the confusion shall be gone.

FIELDING POSITIONS

In regard to fielding, the word—deep—means closer to the boundary. The terms short and silly are used to mean the opposite of deep. The diagram given below gives the names and locations of the various fielding positions. The knowledge of these commonly referred to positions is sure to prove useful not only while playing the game but also while watching a game on television or while listening to commentary on radio. Remember that all these positions are for a right-handed batsman.

BOWLING

When a bowled cricket ball has its first bounce, it is said to have pitched. Different terms are used for the line which the ball pitches on and how far up the pitch it lands. It is generally called length. The exact lengths may vary depending on the speed of the pitch.

Short of Length

A ball bowled without a plan or the one seaming or swinging extravagantly is called a bad ball for the bowler and a good run-scoring ball for the batsman who wil l play off the back foot. (see page 81)

Half Volley

A good length for a batsman to play a drive.

Full Toss

This ball doesn't actually pitch. A low full-toss ball is often hard to be hit. It can be useful in some limited-over games as it may surprise the batsman. But a medium-height full-toss ball is a boon for a tactful batsman.

Short-pitched Ball

It is a delivery in which the ball pitches short of the batsman—often half way up the pitch. It usually becomes a bouncer.

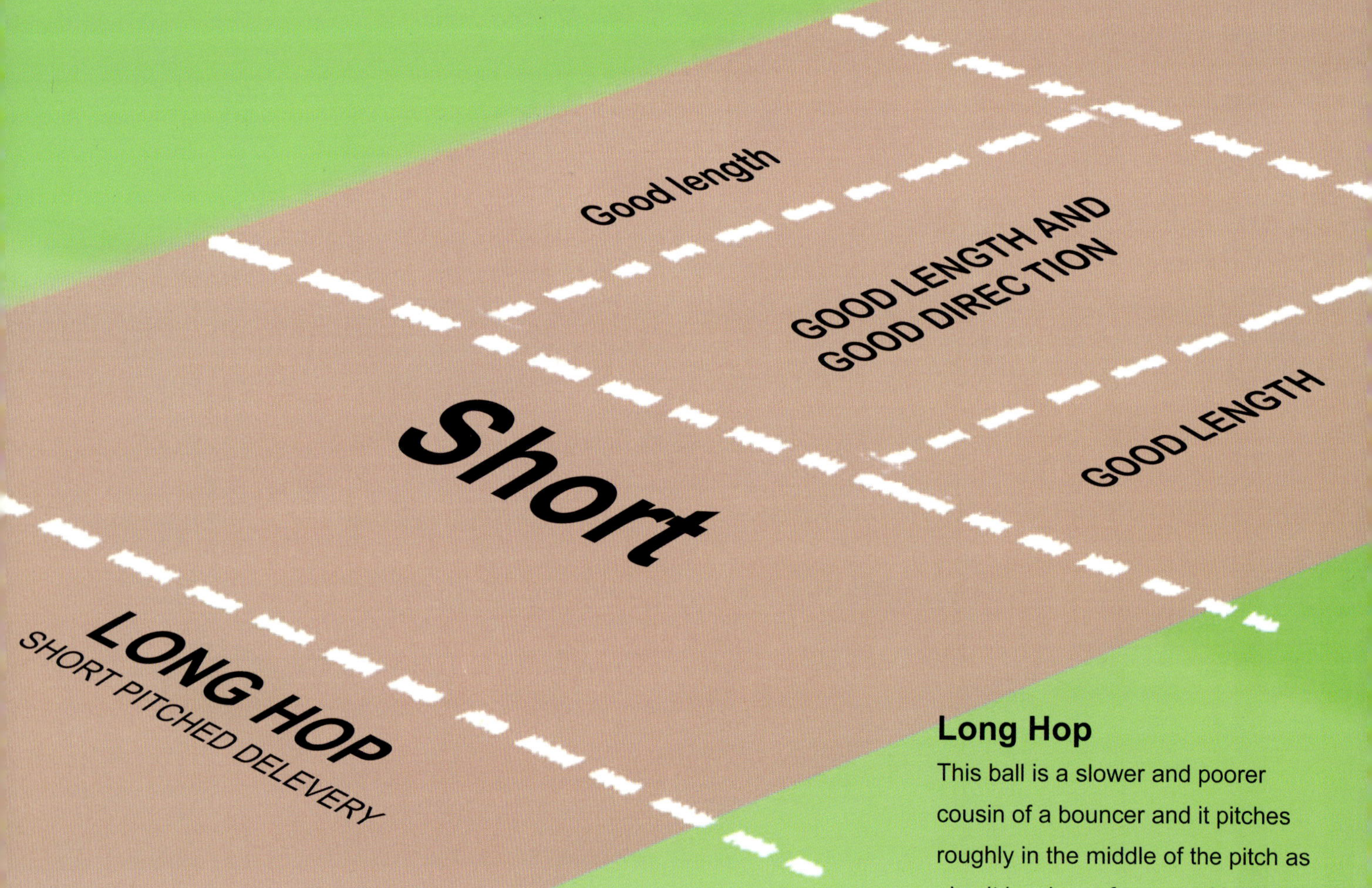

Long Hop

This ball is a slower and poorer cousin of a bouncer and it pitches roughly in the middle of the pitch as also it is a boon for a good batsman.

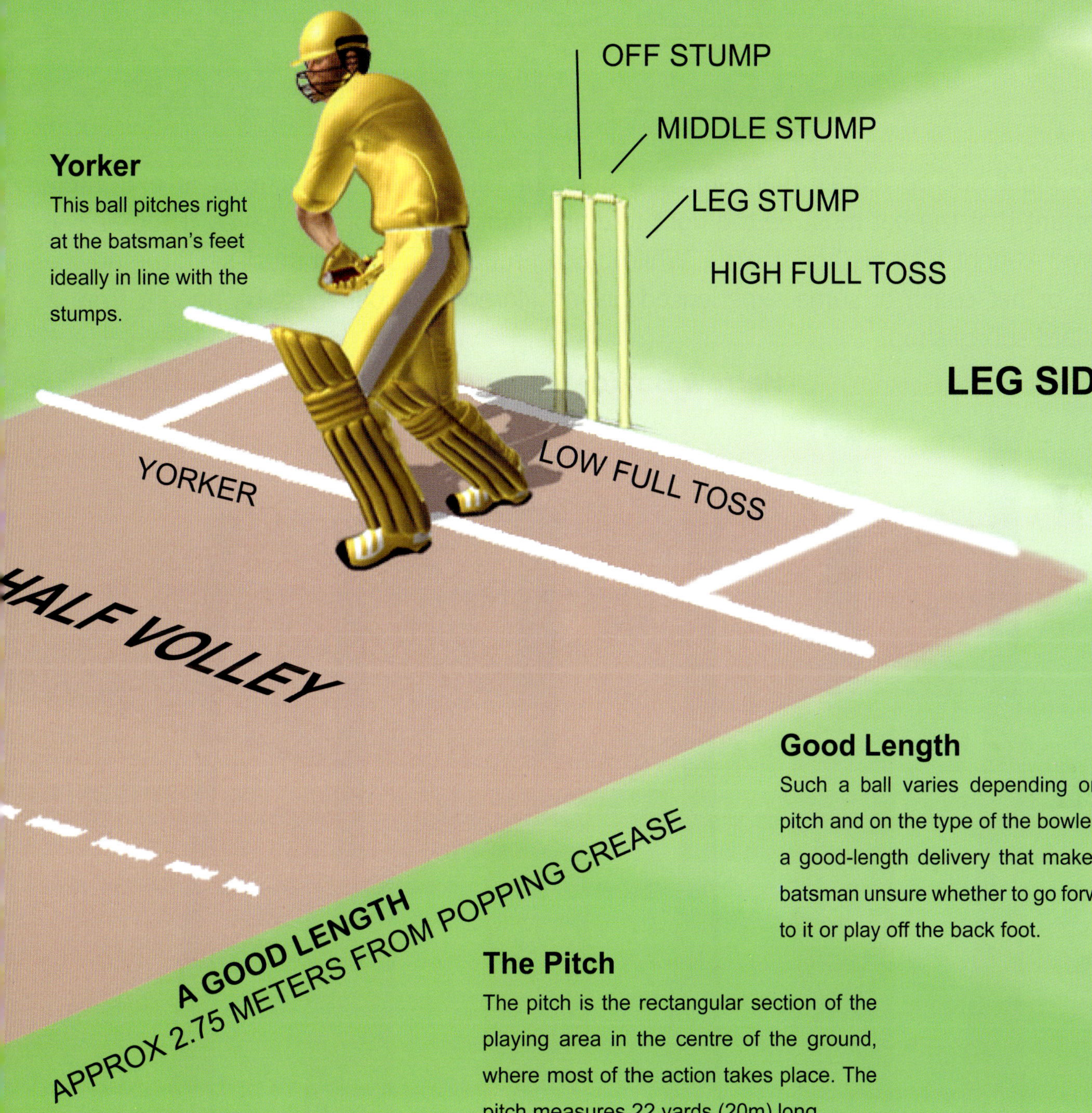

Yorker

This ball pitches right at the batsman's feet ideally in line with the stumps.

Good Length

Such a ball varies depending on the pitch and on the type of the bowler. It is a good-length delivery that makes the batsman unsure whether to go forwards to it or play off the back foot.

The Pitch

The pitch is the rectangular section of the playing area in the centre of the ground, where most of the action takes place. The pitch measures 22 yards (20m) long.

BAT 'n' BALL

A cricket ground is just incomplete if it is without the hitting sound of leather (a ball) on willow (a bat) or it is without leather on shin, i.e. pads worn on legs. A bat and a ball are the essential tools for a game of cricket.

BAT

A bat must not be longer than 96.5 cm and not wider than 10.8 cm. It is extremely important that the bat must be the right size and right weight for the player. If too heavy, a player cannot play his/her strokes. While buying a bat, a batsman must seek the advice of his or her coach or some experienced player. Moreover, a bat must be bought from a standard sports shop.

Harrow Bat for teenagers

Full-size bat **Mongoose Bat**

BALL

The cricket ball is the most important item in the entire sports world. A high-quality ball is made of innermost layers of cork covered by a stitched tight continuous seam all around it. The seam is vital to bowling. But equally vital is the shine of the ball in one side to enable it to swing when bowled.

BAT 'n' BALL CONTROVERSY

There are bats that are wider than the allowed width. Some bats are made of aluminiun. Apart from it, some players are blamed for roughing up the ball with bottle tops and sand. It is called ball-tampering.

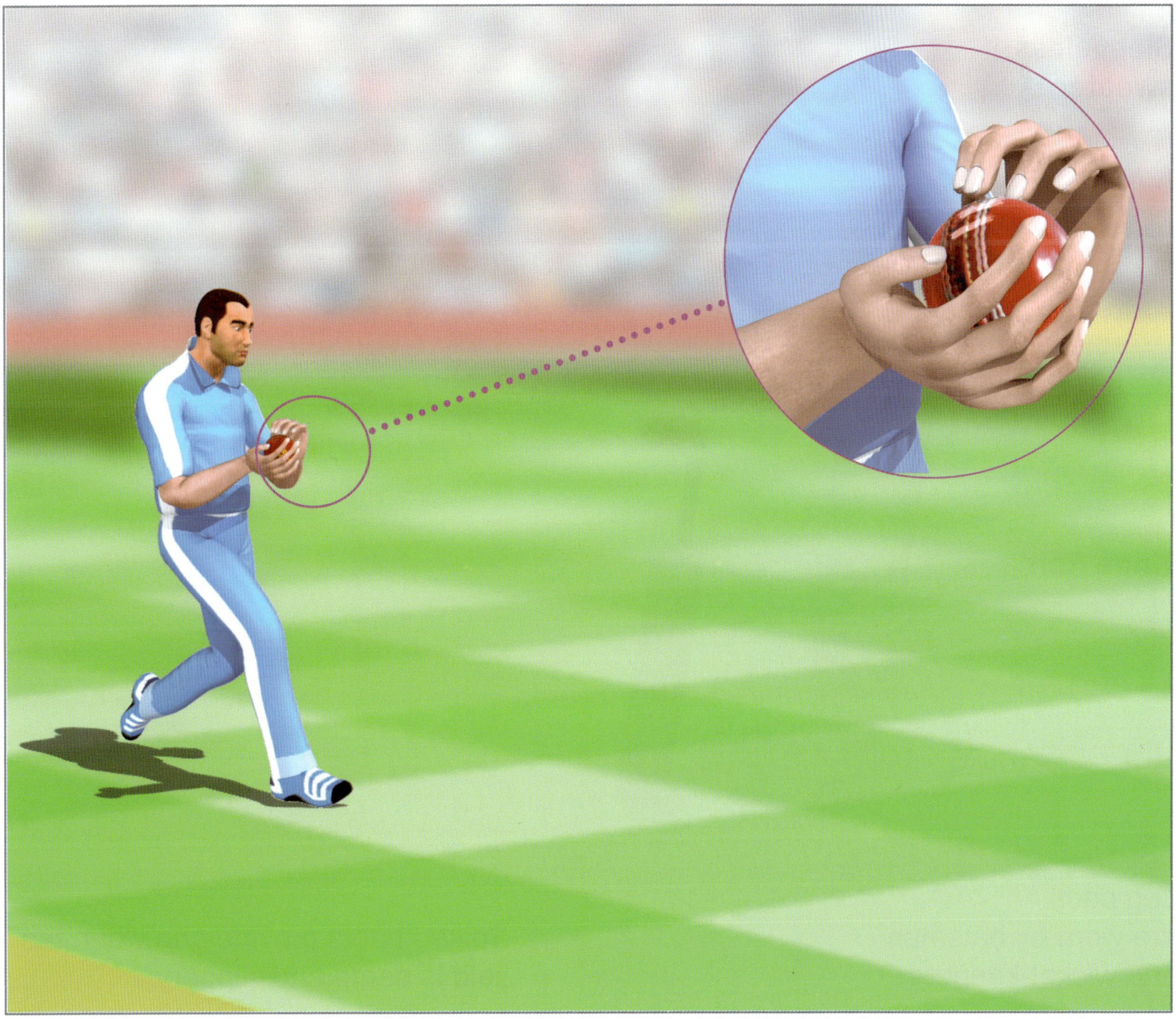

THE CRICKET KIT

White clothes are generally considered good to be used by cricketers, though lately different colours have been adopted by teams of various countries. As for most schools and junior clubs, white T-shirts and light-coloured trousers are allowed. Whatever the clothing may be, it must be comfortably loose so that it may allow full easy movement of all the body-parts. Remember that the clothes must be washed immediately after each game without waiting for the next game. A sleeveless sweater is very useful to put on over the T-shirt.

EQUIPMENT

The pictures given below show other equipments for a cricket player. Remember that the bat needs oiling after regular intervals as per the advice of the seller from whom it has been bought.Perro et fugitatem im lat que estem exeror sam, occuptatem. Am, ut aligent ut optur, que sequi

Protective gloves are vital for batsmen.

A helmet with a protective grill or visor made of tough plastics in front.

Guards and protective padding are worn by batsmen while facing very fast bowlers.

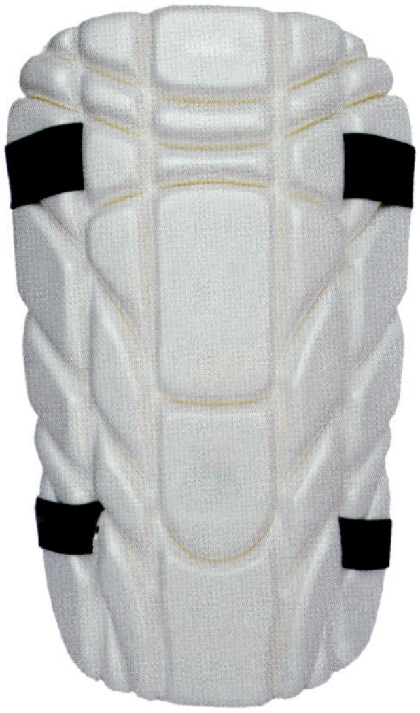

Chest-guard

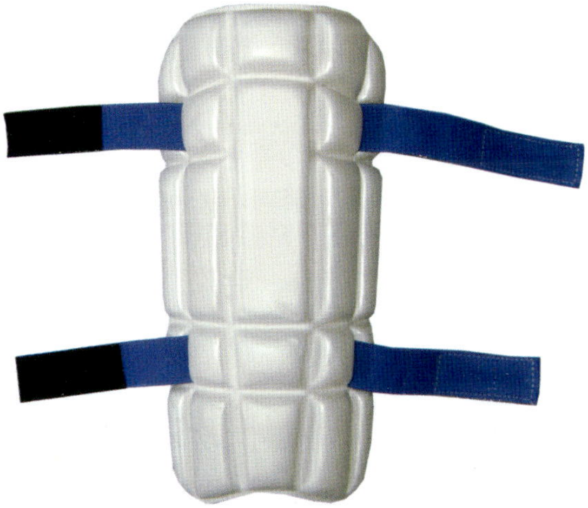

Arm-guard

Thigh guard.

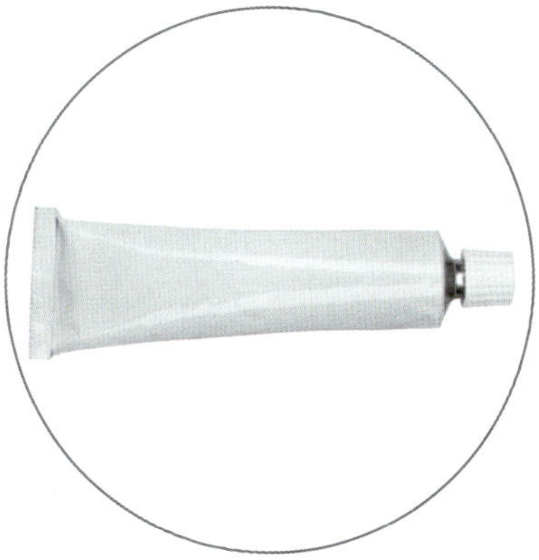

Sun-block is vital when you are in the sun all day.

Chapter Two

Playing The game

KEEPING FIT

Modern Cricket is a game for committed athletes. So you are required to be fighting fit for each game in order to deliver your best performance. Fitness is the foundation at which the ability of bowling, fielding, running between the wickets, catching and general alertness during the game depends.

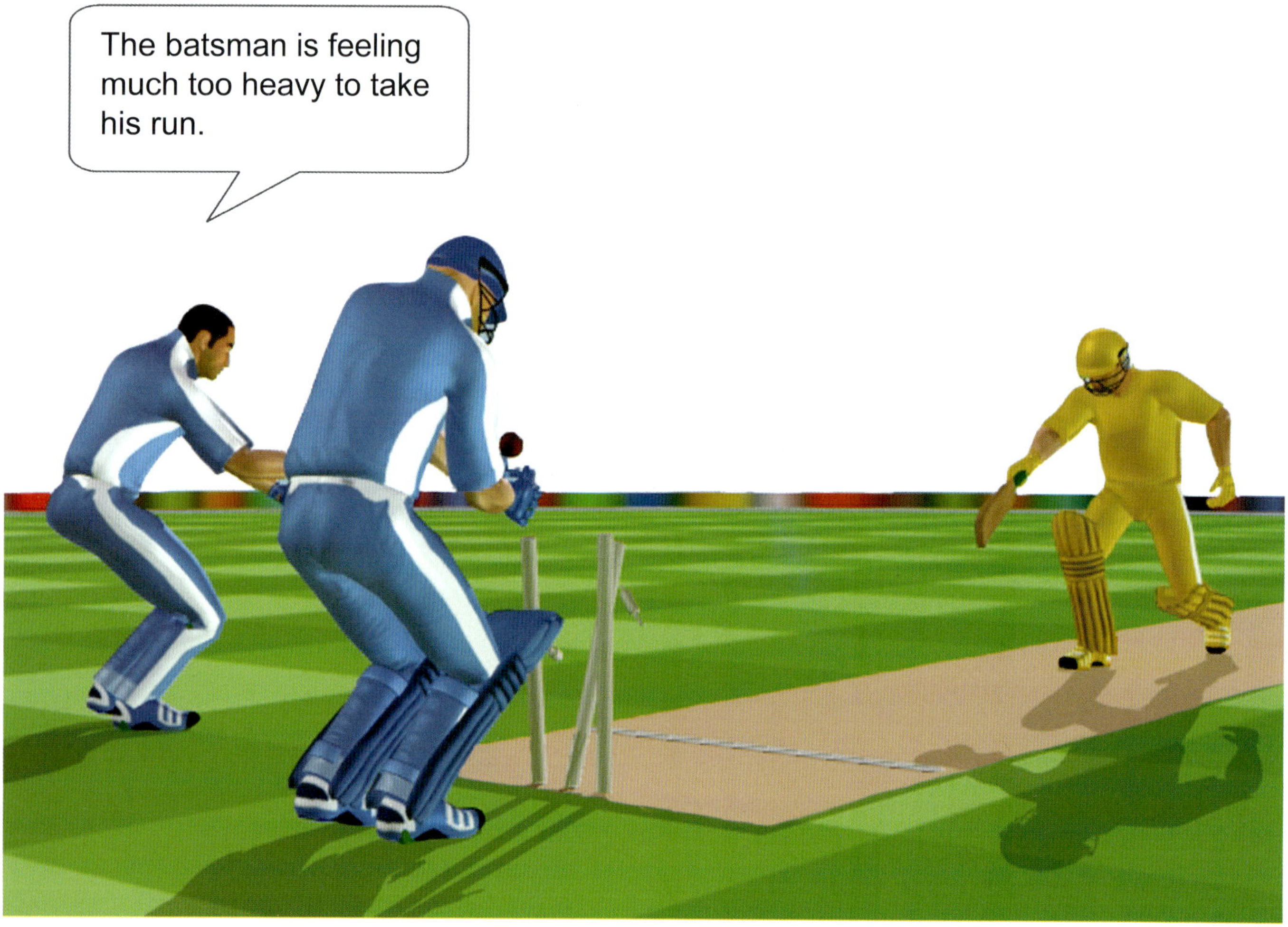

DIET

Best players are very mindful of planned diets. Eating sensibly and avoiding heavy meals are the key-notes of the diet of a true cricketer. Heavy eating stands in the way of running wherever it is needed, i.e. for batsmen, bowlers and fielders equally.

While on the field, especially on a warm day, take full advantage of drinks-breaks. Take in plenty of water, squash or juice to make good the outcoming sweat. But avoid fizzy drinks strictly.

WARM-UPS

A warm-up is highly essential for any cricketer before a game. Light jogging, some fielding exercises and catch attempts undoubtedly push the body and the mind physically and psychologically into the impending game.

Turn right and left with bent elbows but fixed feet

Raise each leg grabbing the foot with each hand in turn

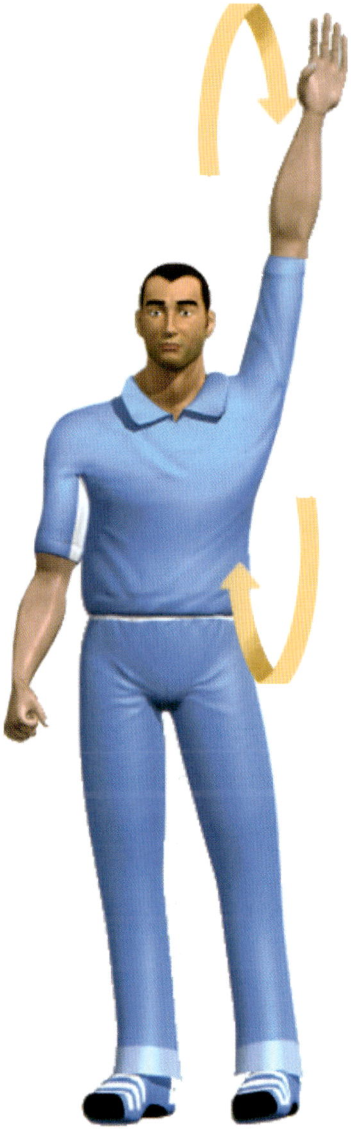

Stretch arms up alternately

Bowlers have a routine of involved stretches before coming to bowl .
You can seek advice from an experienced.

Wicket-keepers keep performing stretching routines even during a match whenever possible. It keeps the body flexible and facilitates bending and moving jobs. Batting for long and wicket-keeping throughout the innings are tough tiring jobs. They require your body and mind fully into the game through repeated stretches.

PRACTICE

A top cricketer, when in form, performs well making the game look easy for others. But the reality is just otherwise. Never be taken in. His or her good performance is not a chance happening. It has hours of hard work and practice behind it. Hard work is the key to success. This saying holds good undoubtedly for the game of cricket, i.e. the more hard-work one puts in, the better performance one will show.

The best time to hone one's batting and bowling skills is a net-session. One must not participate in a net-session half-heartedly, nor take it lightly. A net-session is like a real game one must throw oneself heart and soul into it working on particular features of the game. Top cricketers like Tendulkar, Brian Lara, and Shane Warne never took their net-practice mockingly. Why should anyone else, then?

BE YOUR OWN COACH

Nobody can undermine the importance of a coach at the nets. But if he/she is not around, one must learn to be one's own coach. They say that experience is the greatest teacher. So one must think over each ball to be faced or bowled and pin-point one's wrong act and rectify the next time. If one is right, more practice should be put in because mastery lies in self-correction indeed.

GO IN FOR FANCY MOVES

A player must never be satisfied to be a cricketer in name only. He/She should go in for fancy moves that the top players do. Be it a delivery or a shot, the player must venture to go for it. But it should not be done directly for the first time in a real match. It should be tried out during net practice or small games between mates. One must go for it in a real match when one has mastered it. Nor should it be done under pressure. If done, one is sure to let oneself as well as one's team down.

WHEN NOT AT THE NETS

It is in proper net-sessions only that one can sharpen one's batting and bowling skills. Mind that it needs great sense when one is practising with one's friends away from the proper nets. Practice should be done at a place away from passers-by and from homes. Anyone may play an attacking shot under an impulse and the ball may hit a person, a vehicle or a window-pane. Every move in cricket needs sense, space and practice to get into the line. And the judgement when to play or to leave a delivery or to treat it with a defensive stroke or push is very essential.

OUT !

Each batsman stays on the crease till he/she is declared to be out by the umpire. There are ten different ways in which a batsman can be out. A true batsman tries his/her best to avoid them while a good fielder tries his/her best to make it happen. Given below are these ten different ways one by one.

BOWLED

When the bowler's delivery directly hits the wicket and dislodges a bail which must fall from the top of stumps.

CAUGHT

When the ball, after coming off the bat, is caught by any fielder before it hits the ground but within boundary line rope. If the fielder steps on/over the boundary line, the batsman is not out and also gets six runs as his award.

HIT-WICKET

In playing a shot or starting of for the first run, the batsman breaks the wicket with any part of his body or his equipment including his helmet and spectacles.

STUMPED

The batsman is stumped out if the wicket-keeper breaks the wicket after the batsman has missed the ball but is not able to get his bat, foot or any other body-part on the ground inside the popping crease.

HANDLED BALL

If the batsman deliberately handles the ball with his hand not holding the bat without permission from the other side, he is declared to be out.

THREE RARE 'UNS'

1. Obstructing the field: when a batsman deliberately obstructs a fielder by word or action.
2 Hitting the, ball twice: except when the batsman is defending the wicket from the ball.
3. Timed out: when a new batsman fails to reach the field in a set time after a wicket has fallen.

LBW

It stands for Leg Before Wicket. According to it, a batsman is out if any part of his body stops the ball from hitting the wicket. It is the biggest grey area in cricket and the way of getting out that is far more controversial than all the other rules put together. It is a bit complicated too. So let us view some common situations:

1. The ball pitches outside the leg stump, no matter what, the batsman cannot be given out LBW.

2. The ball hits the batsman on or above the knee roll, it is very likely to be given out because the ball would probably have passed over the stumps.

3. The ball touches the bat before pad ; not out.

4. The batsman attempting a shot can be out if the ball—

(a) Pitches in a straight line between the wickets.

(b) Pitches on off-side of the wicket and the bats man is in line between the wickets.

(c) Hits the batsman before it hits the ground.

5. The batsman, if not playing a shot, can be out whenever the ball strikes him if the umpire believes that the ball would have hit the stumps. But he/she cannot be given out if the ball pitches outside the leg-stump.

RUN OUT

The ball being live, the batsman's foot or bat is not on the ground within the popping crease and the wicket is broken by the ball, the batsman is out. But there are exceptions as well. The safest key-point for the batsman is to lead with his bat grounded while reaching the crease if the run seems tight.

The batsman is run out as his bat is not grounded.

THE UMPIRE

Unlike officials in many other sports, umpires in cricket are still respected and treated well and so they should be indeed as umpiring is a tough job. The umpire has a large range of responsibilities. Let us look at some of them briefly.

SIGNALS

Umpires make a number of signals to players, spectators and the scorers. The commonest signals have been shown at the bottoms of the pages.

LIGHT & WEATHER

Umpires are responsible for deciding whether light and weather conditions are suitable for a game to start or to continue. While feeling frustrated due to a game ending earlier, bear in mind that the umpires are better lovers of the game and they never want to see a game not completed. They announce the teams to be off the pitch only because they earnestly, feel that the conditions are unfair or dangerous for the players.

Out Wide No-ball Bye Leg bye

THE THIRD UMPIRE

Popularity of television and one-day games had put far more pressure on umpires and the use of a third umpire came to be introduced in top-class games. If any regular umpire is not able to decide a catch or run-out, he may signal for the third umpire to watch a TV-replay and signal the result back to the umpires on the field.

APPEALS

The fielding side makes an appeal to the umpire that a batsman must be declared out when they are sure about it. Sometimes an umpire has to suffer modern-day appeals unfairly because they involve uproars like HOW IS THAT ? But the umpires do not give in to these uproars and try to be as fair as possible. A good fielder always respects the decision of an umpire even if he doesn't approve of it and concentrates on the next move.

In the Decision Review System (DRS), each team gets two chances to challenge an umpire's decision. The feilding team captain or the batsman being dismissed invokes the challenge by signaling 'T' with the arm. The system makes the best possible use of the 'Hawk Eye' a ball tracker, a super-slow motion camera and a stump microphone to give the correct decision.

WARNINGS

Sometimes the umpire has to warn a player. For example—

(a) if a batsman opposes when he has been declared to be out.

(b) a bowler repeatedly bowls bouncers.

(c) a bowler steps down the pitch while following through

A good cricketer always acts up to the instructions of the umpire without any comment.

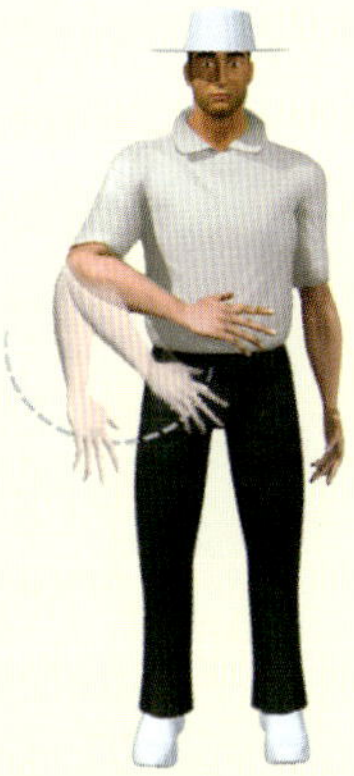

Boundary 4

Boundary 6

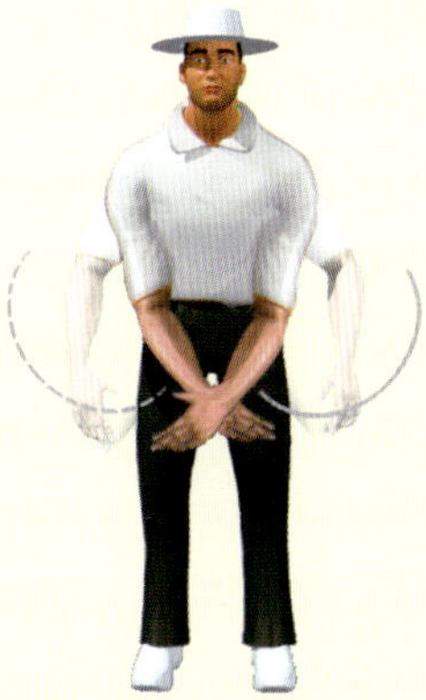

Dead ball

Short run

RUNNING BETWEEN THE WICKETS

Good running between the wickets results from smooth communication between the batsmen on the crease. Generally the batsman playing the ball makes the call whether to take a run or not. But when the ball is played behind the batsman, the other (non-striker) batsman makes the call. The call must be clear and loud in the form of a **YES** or **NO** or **WAIT,** if pausing to see whether the ball gets past the fielder. It is not wise to go in for a run if it can't be made safely. Mind that a run-out is sheer waste of a wicket.

As the bowler comes to bowl, the non-striker batsman should keep his bat grounded behind him but start walking forwards. This activity is called **backing up**.

EXTRAS

Extra runs can be scored even without hitting the ball. There are four types of extra runs—**wides**, **byes, leg byes** and **no-balls**.

If a bowler bowls a ball too wide or too high for a shot to be attempted, the umpire signals a **wide**. It causes one run to be added to the score and the ball must also be bowled again.

If the batsman doesn't hit the ball but the ball is not gathered by the fielding side, the batsman can take runs called byes. If the ball comes off the batsman's body (usually the leg) when he is attempting a shot or avoiding a beamer or a bouncer, the extra runs are called **leg-byes**.

A **no-ball*** is signalled by the empire if the bowler's feet do not land in the proper area. One run is added to the score and the bowler has also to bowl the ball again.

*In Britain Country Championship, a no ball, adds two runs to the score.

Chapter Three

Batting Basics

HOLDING THE BAT

A left-handed batsman should hold the bat with his right hand on top and wrap both the hands around the upper part of the bat-handle. The hands should be quite close to each other so that they may work together. The thumb and the first finger of either hand should make a V-shape and must be in line with each other. Moreover, they should be facing away from the batsman's body.

As for a right-handed batsman, he or she should follow all the above instructions with the difference that the left hand will be on top.

THE GRIP

The bat must be gripped firmly with the hand on top. As for the other hand, the grip is to be a bit loose for proper adjustments.

The top hand is responsible for keeping the ball down during most shots. So firmness of its grip is very, very important.

One must concentrate on one's grip frequently to see whether that is perfectly right.

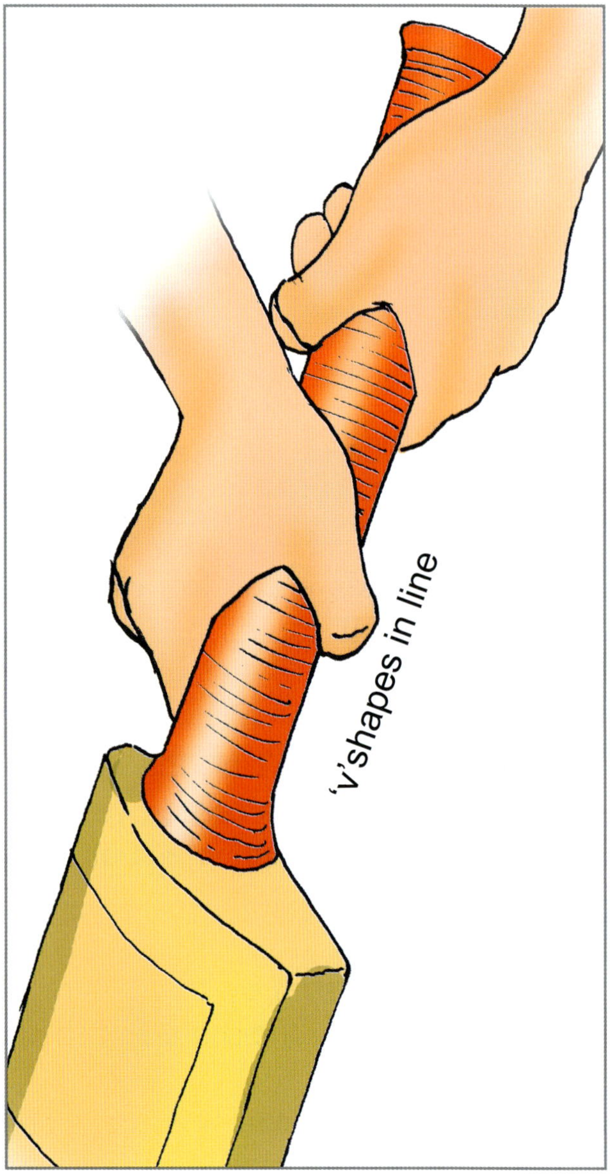

STANCE

The rules regarding stance are varied indeed. But to begin with, the basic stable side on stance should be adopted as it serves most of the batsmen well. Remember that the stance must be natural and quite comfortable.

Both feet on either sides of the crease and 15-25 cm apart.

A TOP-CLASS TIP :
Don't crouch ; stand tall. To achieve this, rest your bat on the toe of you back-foot, not on the ground.

BACK-LIFT

In order to hit a decent shot, the back-lift must be smooth and relaxed. This fact about the back-lift must never be under-estimated or over-looked. Keeping the bat grounded, the top hand has to do all the work here. Head and feet must be still and the bat should swing back in a straight line over the stumps. Using the wrists, face of the bat must be opened a bit.

Head and eyes remain straight

Some batsmen bring the bat back at an angle past the off-stump. But others like to play with a truly high back-lift. To begin with, it is wise to stick to the classical back-lift as shown above. Most batsmen find it easier and more effective as well.

WHEN TO ACT ?

As soon as the bowler starts bringing the bowling arm up, start your back-lift. If late, the stroke will have to be made in a rush. If too early, the ball will keep hanging and the shot may get mis-timed.

BACK-LIFT S.O.S. :

Straight   Open   Smooth

USING A MIRROR

Grip, stance and back-lift are the three basics of batting and so that are vital to good batting. Practise hard and so much so that they become your second nature. You can use a full length mirror and practise in front of it to check your positioning and movements.

THE NIGHT-WATCHMAN

In top-ranking matches, a lower but trustworthy batsman is put ahead of higher players when a wicket falls shortly before the end of a day's play. Such a batsman is called a night-watchman as he is supposed to stick to the crease in order to protect the better batsman till the start of the next day's play.

Some night watchmen make a real nuisance of themselves by staying on the crease for quite some time. It requires a lot of practice indeed.

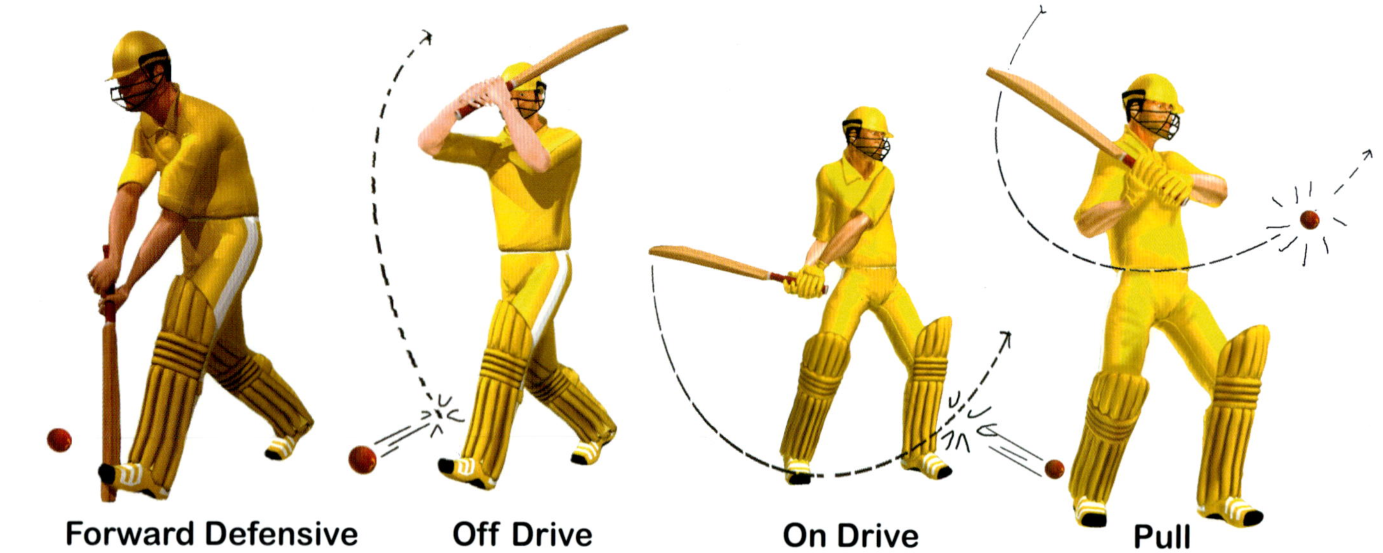

Forward Defensive Off Drive On Drive Pull

Sweep Cut off front foot Back defensive Hook

GOING IN TO BAT

The above pictures show eight different types of shots that should be mastered by a good batsman to the extent that each of them should be at his command. It will surely enable him/her to play the one that is most suited to the ball and the conditions he is facing at a certain time.

A good batsman is always keen to make runs. But staying on the crease is essential for it. It is possible only if you are able to protect your wicket. And for it, you must be good at defensive shots, i.e. wise enough to decide as to when to play a shot and when to leave a ball undisturbed. Remember that no penalty is there for letting a ball go. Experienced batsmen are master hands at deciding which ball to play and which one to let go. For example, a poor ball wide of the off-stump must be left out with a view to staying at the crease and not aiming at scoring. But if scoring is the priority, such a ball has to be punished with a forceful square cut.

BALL WATCHING

The skill to watch the ball in the bowler's hand before he releases it is highly useful to become a good batsman. Keep your eyes constantly at the ball after it has left the bowler's hand.

Watching the ball travelling towards you, it must be instantly worked out where it is going to pitch and how you are to deal with it. Some deliveries, such as a slow weak bouncer digging in just half-way up the pitch, can be easily spotted while some others can't. Only experience can help you to delve into the bowler's art, i.e. to pick the line and the length of a delivery well in time and then deal with it effectively.

TAKING GUARD

When a batsman first comes to the wicket, the umpire is there to help him or her get in the right position in front of the stumps. This is what we call taking guard. So the batsman may ask the umpire for a guard in line with the middle stump, the leg-stump or the middle and leg-stump. Once in line, the batsman can make a scratch on the ground at this place and use it as a guiding mark.

FOOT-WORK

Many strokes depend on the batsman's adjusting his/her feet either to get to the pitch of the ball or to get the rest of the body in a suitable position to play the stroke. It is vital to work on it carefully. Lazy or poor foot-work leads to an out again and again.

FORWARD DEFENSIVE

A good-length delivery heading towards the wicket should be played using a forward defensive stroke which proves great for a single-run score to begin with. Then it serves as a basis of major run-scoring shots—forward drives. In the absence of this forward defensive stroke, a batsman cannot stay on the crease for long.

The batsman's head and front shoulder lead him or her into the stroke.

The front knee should be bent to support the body-weight forwards while the hind leg is extended with the foot on the ground inside the crease.

The back foot must be kept behind the crease failing which the ball may go through and the batsman may be stumped by the wicket-keeper.

The batsman's front must be as near the pitch of the ball as possible.

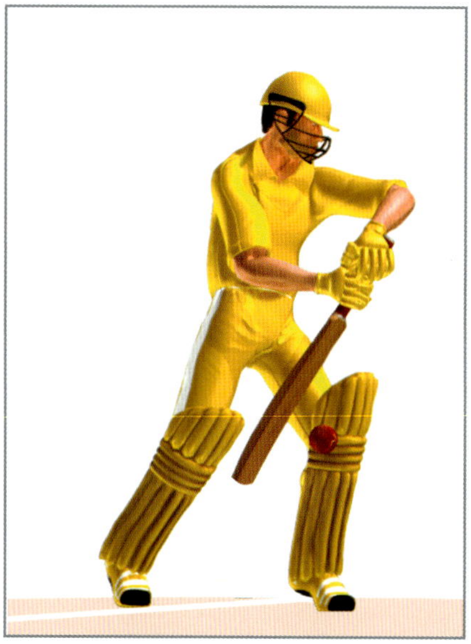

The top-hand must be fully in control of the bat while the bottom hand's grip should be gentle. Together, they must cushion the ball just as it comes onto the bat.

The batsman must never push forwards before picking up the line of delivery.

The handle of the bat must be angled ahead of its blade.

The batsman's front pad and bat form a barrier against the ball tending to go past.

GETTING FORWARDS

The forward shots must be practised a lot with someone bowling full-length deliveries. It should be ensured that the ball comes to rest within five paces after being cushioned well.

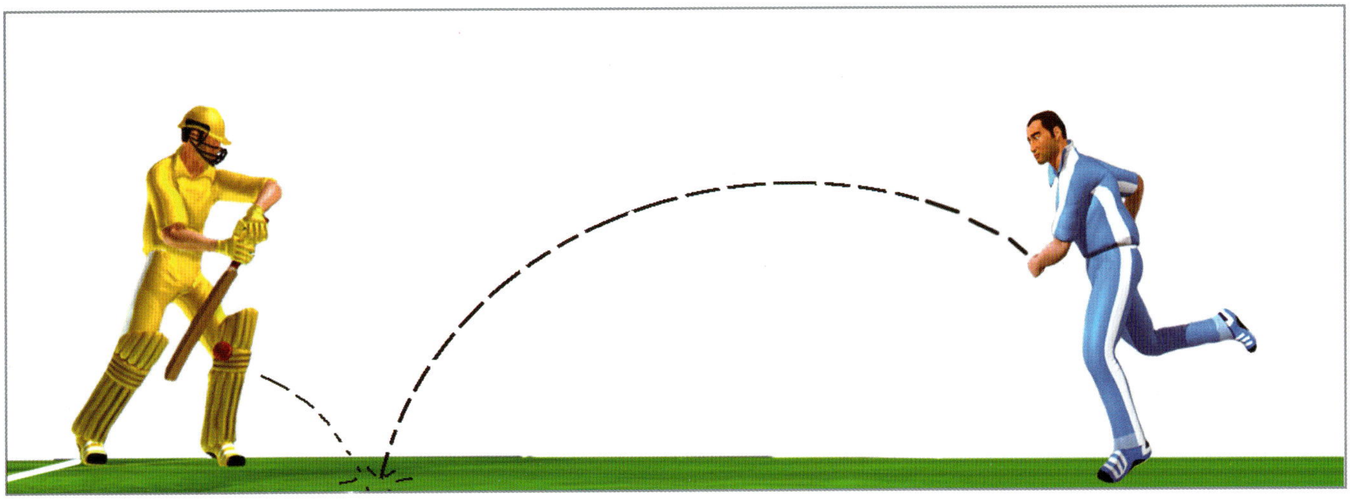

PLAYING WITH SOFT HANDS

Playing with soft hands is the greatest compliment to a batsman for a number of shots. It means that the batsman's grip is not rigid but gentle enough to allow him to guide and drop the ball after his own will.

BACKWARD DEFENSIVE

Playing off the back-foot is a bit harder than playing off the front foot. Using the entire crease enables a batsman to defend the wicket against a rising fast ball or an awkward delivery that has been pitched just short-of-length. Not only this, it may allow the batsman to tuck a ball away and get runs. Stepping back into the crease gives the batsman more time to play the shot.

As the ball pitches, the batsman must step back and across keeping the back foot parallel to the batting crease. Then he/she must step across towards off-stump and get his or her shoulder just inside the line of the ball.

Staying in perfect balance the batsman should draw his/her front foot to the heel of the back foot and put all the body-weight on the back foot but keeping the head over the ball and maintaining the body-balance with the front foot.

BACKWARD DEFENSIVE

A batsman batting down the order must not give up easily believing that his/her runs may turn the game. The team may need the batsman to remain on the crease as long as possible to score the much-needed runs or to hit out for the vital extra runs. In such cases, the fellow- batsman is generally a senior batsman. So the longer the lower batsman stays around, the more balls he can face to add to the score.

DOWN THE ORDER

Just like the forward defensive, the backward defensive must also be practised a lot. One can practise one's positioning and the footwork even without a ball. The footwork should be practised to the extent that it becomes a second nature. It is sure to enable a batsman to concentrate on the ball and also on the movements of his/her body and the arm.

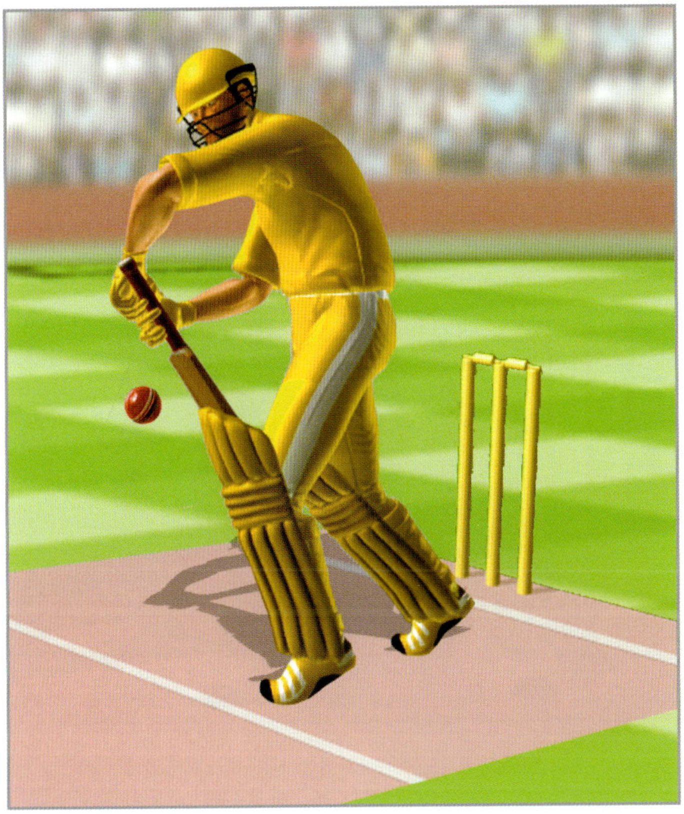

The batsman should keep his/her top hand well in front of the bottom hand. The front elbow should be raised nicely high.

The batsman should angle the bat and but must not follow through to keep the ball down. His/Her eyes must be on the ball throughout the stroke peering over or around the bat-handle.

AVOIDING A BOUNCER

A bouncer is a short-pitched delivery that rises high towards the batsman's head or the upper body. Experienced players sometimes play hook-shots to bouncers. Such shots need great skill and a lot of confidence indeed. So it is best to try to avoid playing such a shot and save oneself from the ball swaying out of its reach or ducking oneself beneath the ball itself. Keeping the eyes fixed on the movement of the ball is of vital importance.

TURNING DEFENCE INTO ATTACK

With proper practice, any batsman can turn his defensive shots—both forward and backward—into aggressive shots and score runs.

THE FORWARD PUSH

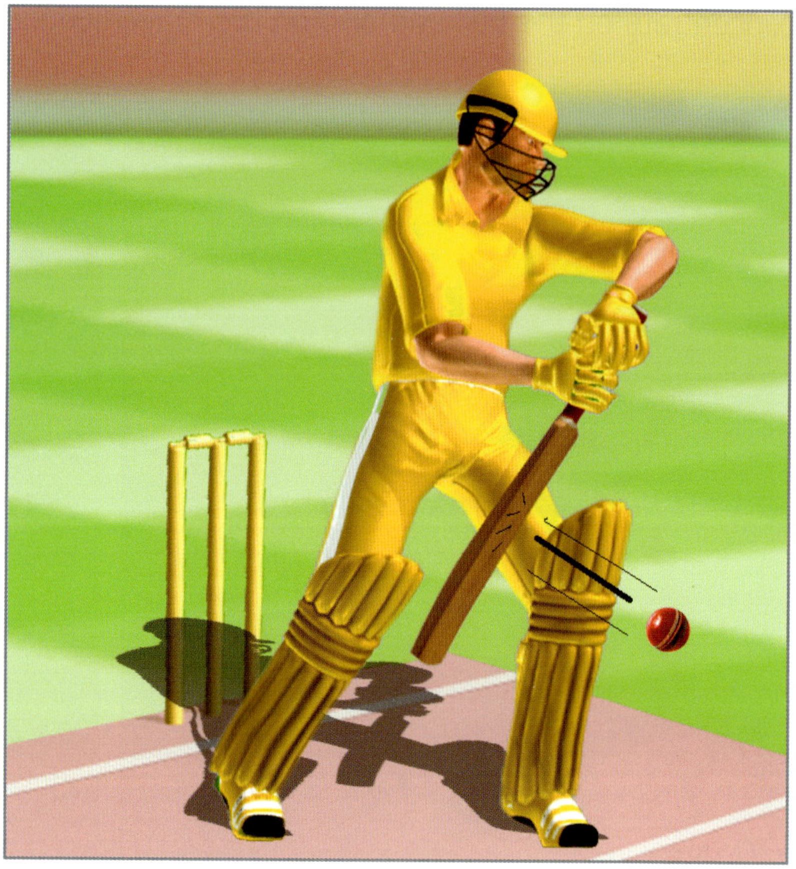

If the fielders are located in the outfield with a view to stopping boundaries, there is always space near the batsman where he/she can push the ball and pick up singles or doubles. In such a case, a forward defensive shot is used as a basis. But two things are required to be done :

(a) The bat must be angled right or left to nudge the ball into the space.

(b) Playing softly, the ball must be pushed firmly with the bat.

PUSH DRILL

The batsman must mark out two or three 4m square target-areas on the off-side nearly 12 to 25 metres away. Asking a friend to bowl and another to field, he/she must try to nudge the ball so that it goes into one of those target areas. 5 points per delivery should be scored for a ball that goes into the target area and one point for a ball that rests three paces away from the target area. Facing two overs, the friends must be switched over.

BACK-FOOT FORCING SHOT

A batsman can turn the backward short into a run-scoring stroke. The footwork is the same as the forward push but the back-foot should be well in the crease, with the line of the off-stump. The front elbow should rise up in the line with the ball, while the bottom hand should rent loose on the handle as shown in the picture.

SETTING TARGETS

It is desirable for a new batsman to set himself/herself small achievable targets—batting for a number of overs to reach double figures. A few selected basic shots should be practised and developed till the batsman is able to play them with confidence. The result of the forward and backward defensive shots plus one or two run-scoring shots will be amazing indeed.

Chapter Four

Learning To Bowl

BOWLING BASICS

The action of bowling is an unnatural and apparently illogical one. The bolwing action is built on three foundation: momention, balance and timing. Whatever the type of bowler one is or one wants to be (from pace bowler to off-spinner), bowling a ball involves four stages. They are—grip, run-up, delivery, follow through, we are explaining here these stages one by one in regard to a right-handed medium-paced bowler. It is perhaps the most likely type that most bowlers starts out as.

ASIC GRIP

This grip works for fast bowlers and medium-paced bowlers. It is essential that the ball be gripped with fingers, not in the palm of the hand.

More advanced grips that make the ball swing, seam or spin, will be taken up later on.

The first and the middle fingers grip the ball on either side of the seam.

The thumb is at the bottom.

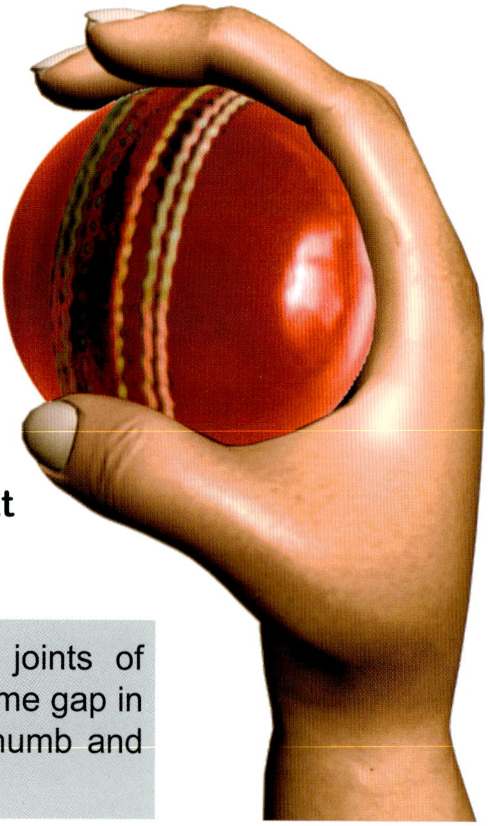

The ball rests on the last joints of fingers. But there must be some gap in the V formed between the thumb and the fingers.

RUN-UP BASICS

The run-up is designed to get the bowler to just the right position from where to bowl. The run-up has to be measured and marked out in advance by the bowler so that he/she may know where to start. The bowler starts his run-up facing the batsman and builds up his/her speed steadily and smoothly.

To begin with, the bowler must not worry about an overlong run-up in order to build up a huge pace. Instead, he/she must grasp the basics which are as under :

(a) The run-up should be smooth.

(b) The bound (leap) in which to turn from front-on to side-on should be made carefully.

(c) The stride taken just before bowling the ball must be quite- balanced. The stride is called the delivery stride.

The bowler's head stays level

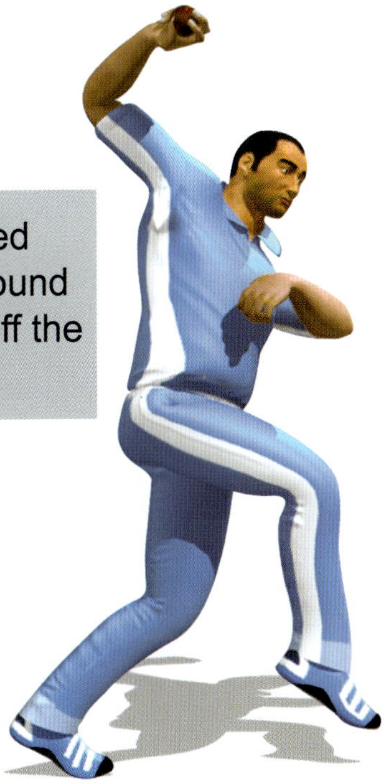

For right-handed bowlers, the bound (leap) comes off the left-foot.

Shoulders sideways pointing down the pitch.

Right-foot turns, so that it may land parallel to the bowling crease.

The bound (leap) is the link between the run-up and the delivery stride.

THE DELIVERY

Whether it is watched live or on TV, a bowler's delivery looks like a flurry of blurred legs and arms. If it is slowed down, it can be watched in a better way and followed what actually goes out. A delivery is a continuous movement but it can be broken into five key stages.

STAGE I

The bound (leap) takes place before the delivery stride. In it, the bowler leaps off his/her left foot and lands with the right foot just behind the bowling crease, the foot being parallel to it. The bound enables the bowler to turn from the front-on position to the side-on position. With it, the bowler's, left arm starts going up.

STAGE II

As the bowler lands from the bound, he/she enters the coil position. The left arm (the front one) is such that it allows him to look over the front shoulder at the batsman and the pitch ahead. The bowling hand is below the chin of the bowler who leans backwards curving the back and getting ready to uncoil and deliver the ball.

STAGE III

Having entered the delivery stride, the bowler uncoils. His/Her left arm points down the pitch, i.e. to the direction in which the ball is to be bowled. The bowler's head also turns along with it and the bowling arm moves over in a high arc.

STAGE IV

Finally, the bowler's left foot lands such that it is just touching or even cutting the crease. If it lands just ahead of the crease, the delivery will be given a no-ball. As soon as the body-weight comes down on the left foot of the bowler, the ball is released with the arm remaining straight and high.

STAGE V

The ball having been released, the bowler allows the bowling arm to move in a circle just past the left hip keeping quite close to the body. In fact, it is part of the follow-through. The eyes of the bowler are at the batsman over the shoulder of the bowling arm that should be pointing down the pitch.

THE FOLLOW THROUGH

A proper follow-through is a must for successful bowling. It has often been seen that bowlers do really hard work but ruin their deliveries only because of a poor follow-through.

After releasing the ball, the bowling arm should not stop dead. If it happens, it is sure to jar the body and cause some injury as well. Above all, it is likely to send the delivery off the target. The proper follow-through demands that the bowling arm should go down right past your body and the bowler's first step should move towards the batsman. The non-bowling arm should pass close to the body and then backwards behind the body.

But the bowler must not go down the pitch more than a couple of strides as a part of follow-through. He/she must complete the follow-through to the side of the pitch but not falling away too quickly after bowling the ball and keeping the body in balance with eyes on the ball.

The bowler must see where the ball lands; what it does after it has pitched and how the batsman responds to it. The ball having been hit may come straight back to the bowler. So he/she must be ready enough to catch it.

The bowler stays alert and it is rewarded with a caught-and-bowled chance.

BOWLING MUST BE NATURAL.

Though bowling involves a lot of technical approach as explained in the previous pages, it is quite a natural action. Things don't always go as the text-books describe them, the bowler may have to act in a slightly different manner using his/her discretion. This is not something for the bowler to fret and frown. He/She may talk to some coach who may guide and suggest some alteration or confirm his/her action to be fine and fruitful.

Some very fast pace bowlers find it difficult to land their feet parallel to the crease on delivery with their feet landing down the pitch instead.

SPLIT-UP PROCEDURE

If a bowler has some problems while following the bowling sequence, he/she must not be disappointed. Instead, the entire sequence should be split into parts that are easily manageable. These parts should be practised one by one separately. Getting mastery of each part, all the parts should be practised together in proper sequence. The problems will be no more. Help can be sought from a good coach for proper guidance.

For example, if a bowler is learning the run-up action for the first time and faces some difficulties in it, the entire approach can be broken. At first marking out the run-up should be taken up without bowling. Then the run-up should be made. Next the feet must be watched carefully, i.e. where they land. It will be a sort of self-coaching through minding one's own actions and questioning oneself as under:

(a) Did I shorten my steps during the last strides?

(b) Did I lengthen my steps during the last strides?

Many bowlers find it more meaningful and beneficial to practise their run-up sequence next to a proper crease and wicket.

LEARN TO SLOW DOWN

A very serious mistake that new bowlers often make is—trying to bowl very fast. It often makes the ball ping off in various directions. Apart from it, the danger of straining a muscle is also there. Work up to it bearing in mind that an accurate slow delivery is far more difficult to be played safely by a batsman than a faster off-target delivery.

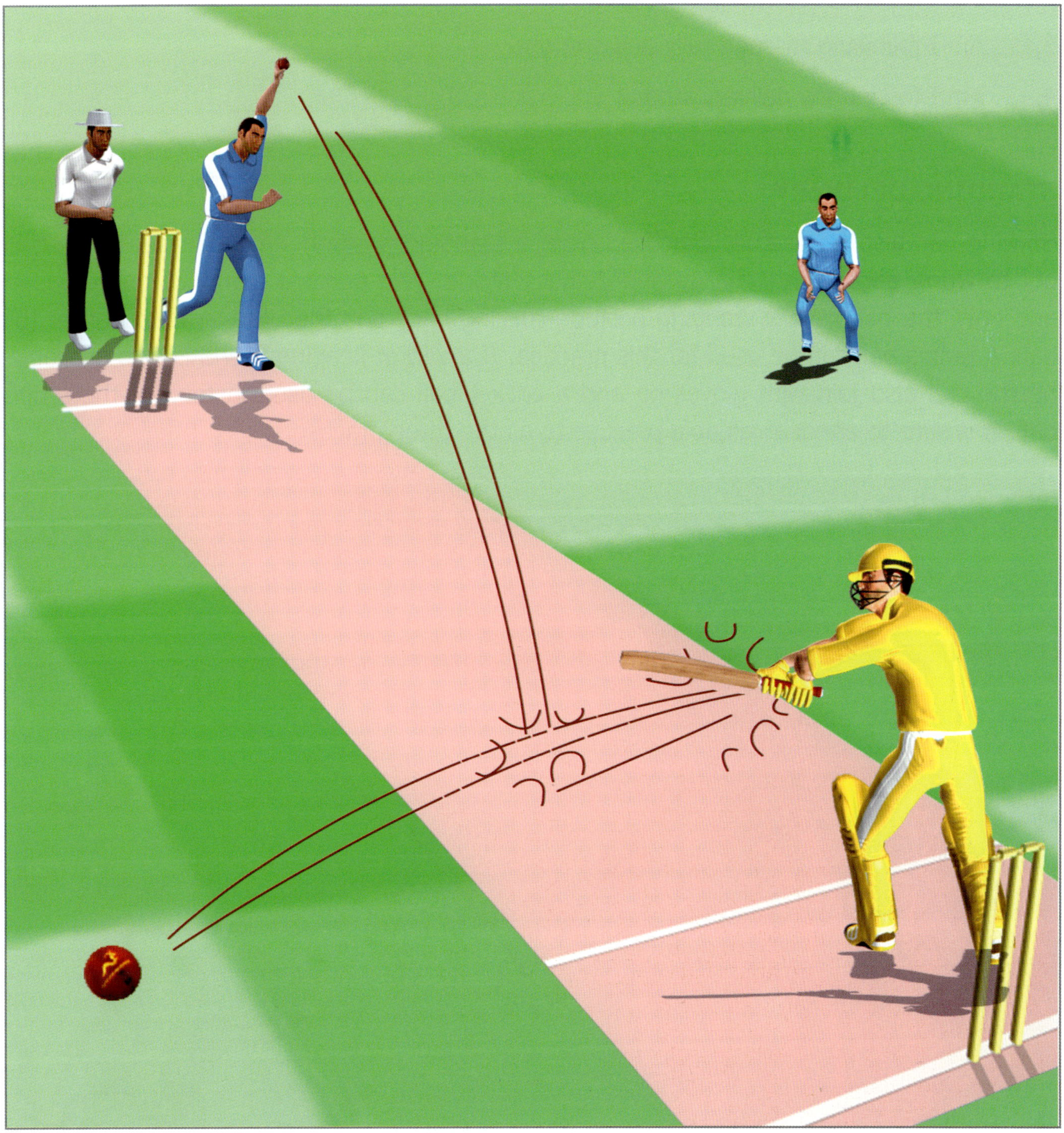

It doesn't matter how fast the delivery is. If it is off the target, any smart batsman can despatch it easily for runs.

BOWLING PRACTICE

The best bowling practice can be done in the nets against real live batsmen. But it can also be done on one's own or even with a friend at a walking pace in front of a mirror. Self-coaching is beneficial when concentrating on the following points:

1. Am I side-on?
2. Are my head and eyes pointing ahead?
3. Am I following through fully and straight?
4. Am I forcing my delivery stride?

STANDING DELIVERY

Bowling can also be usefully practised from a standing position. In this case, one hasn't got to worry about one's run-up and delivery stride. Two persons stand 20 metres apart and bowl the ball from a standing position rocking back and then forwards to deliver the ball. A tennis ball can be used for this practice. If a wicket-keeping friend is also available, he/she can also join with gloves on and a cricket ball can be used instead of the tennis ball. It is sure to effect a valuable practise to all the three practisers:

PITCHING A DELIVERY

Perfect pitching means pitching the ball on target area. Some bowlers in the past perfected their pitching action placing a piece of cloth for the deliveries to land on it. It is sure to create a lot of confidence in the bowler. So it will be very useful to practise landing one's deliveries on a target area starting with a 1.5 metre area and slowly reducing it.

RUN-UP RYTHM

A good rhythm is the key-note of a perfect run-up. A bowler must make up his/her mind before starting the run-up—what type of delivery is to be bowled ? It is sure to provide the bowler with a good chance of concentrating on his/her run-up and the delivery as well.

It is always beneficial to go over a number of paces before approaching the run-up marker. It helps a bowler to shuffle his/her pace and get the foot right on the marker and ensure an accurate run-up.

Having got full control of his or her action, the bowler should build up his/her run-up and his fastest possible speed while reaching the delivery stride. Efforts must be made to bowl close to the stumps in order to get in a straight line to the batsman. After gaining confidence, one may go in for bowling a little wider and vary the delivery-angle.

RUN-UP AND NO-BALLS

It has been explained that a perfect run-up is very significant for being in a good position to deliver the ball. But it remains to be explained yet that a perfect run-up is also required to avoid no-ball deliveries. No-balls are foot-faults of a bowler and are closely related to where the bowler's feet are at the time of releasing the ball.

When an umpire announces a delivery to be a no-ball, one run is added to the score of the batting team and the bowler has to re-bowl the ball. Not only this, if the batsman acts quickly, he can hit the ball to score more runs because he won't be out even if caught or bowled from a no-ball.

FREE HIT

According to the new cricket rules, a no-ball earns the batsman an additional free hit in any direction but in limited-over games only.

POWERPLAY

A powerplay is a rule concerning fielding restriction in One Day International. The first ten overs in an innings are defined as Powerplay One. During this period, only two players are allowed to stand outside the 30-yards circle and two fielders are placed in close catching position. The first block of five overs is defined as Powerplay Two. In this, three fielders are allowed outside the 30-yards circle. There is no mandatory member of close catchess. The second block of five overs is known on Powerplay Three, that has similar parameters to Powerplay Two.

Feet must not touch the
return crease
Rear foot may be on, behind or
in front of the bowling crease.
RETURN CREASE
BOWLING CREASE
POPPING CREASE
Some part of the front foot whether it
is grounded or raised must be behind
the popping crease.

Chapter Five

Fielding

How fielding is to be regarded—a fun or a chore—just depends upon the individual attitude of a player. But the point remains that every player, whether a bowler or a batsman has to do the fielding job. Why not take it as a fun, then ?

Good fielding is of utmost importance so much so that it can turn the fate of a match. Best fielders are generally considered to be all-rounders. In modern cricket, each player has got to be a good fielder. Wherever a fielder is placed in the outfield, the captain wants him or her to concentrate on the ball as soon as it is delivered by the bowler. And if the ball happens to come within the fielder's reach, it should be grabbed. Walking over a few paces just as the bowler delivers the bowl, can help a fielder focus and stay alert.

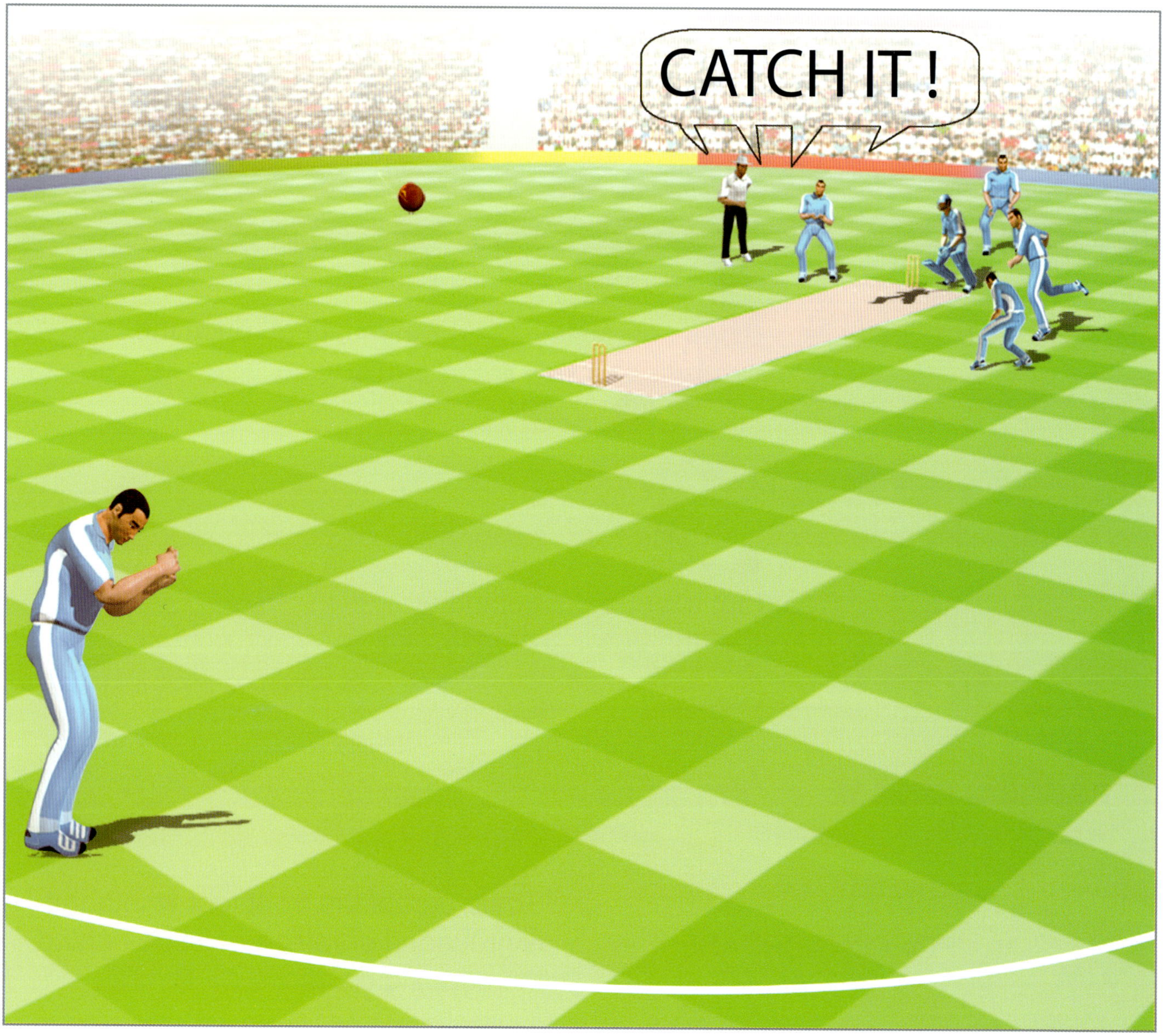

STOPPING AND THROWING

Every fielder wants to be credited with a catch. But catching is less important than stopping the ball and throwing it back. As soon as a fielder sees the ball coming towards him or her, its line should be judged and effort should be made to get behind it. If possible, the fielder must move forwards to intercept it swiftly.

THE LEG BARRIER STOP

Using a leg to obstruct a ball is the most reliable and safest way of stopping a ball coming along the ground. The lower leg and other foot can create an effective wide obstruction for the ball. The fielder should get behind the ball, fall on his / her knees allowing the leg to trail out to its full length and placing the other foot sideways. There must not be any gap between the foot and the bent knee. The hands must be got behind the ball. Thus the leg and the foot are there to act as a second line of defence.

THE THROW IN

The long-barrier stop is naturally followed by a quick pick-up and throw of the ball. As soon as a fielder gets up from the long-barrier stop, he / she should grab the ball in the throwing hand and get ready for a quick throw. Stepping forwards with the front foot, the ball should be thrown with the non-throwing arm pointing ahead as if to act as a guide. The ball should give the wicket-keeper a good chance for a run-out at the other end.

Aiming at the wickets, the ball should be thrown just over the stumps. But if the fielder is much too far away, the ball should be made to reach the wickets after one bounce.

THROW FOOTBALL

Marking two lines about 20 metres apart and placing a light-to-medium weight plastic football in between the lines without stepping over the lines fielders should take turns to throw a tennis ball onto the football trying to knock it over the opponent's line.

CHASE, PICK-UP AND THROW

1. Chase. Often a fielder has to chase a ball hotly in the outfield. While reaching the ball, the fielder's back will be towards the wicket. He/She must take a position with the ball on the side of the throwing arm.

2. Pick-up. The ball which is near the fielder's foot should be picked up staying low and putting the body-weight on the other foot.

3. Throw. Before turning round, the ball should be thrown. All the three efforts must make a single smooth sequence.

This is a move that can be practised with a friend also. The ball, having been picked, should be thrown to him or her to be picked up and thrown over the wickets.

DIVES AND SLIDES

The techniques (moves) already studied are often followed when a fielder has ample time to get in the line of the ball or under it. But the ball is not always co-operative to let the fielder be able to do so. So when the time is much too short, a dive or slide comes in handy to stop the ball. A dive, if possible, certainly saves runs. But a fielder must not injure himself or herself.

A slide is just like a sliding tackle in the game of football. It is performed either through creating a long barrier using the leg or sliding along with the ball and stopping it on its path. Remember that slides and dives are followed by quick recoveries and throw-ins.

FOOTING THE BALL

This move is to be used as the last resort because a foot can create only a very small barrier and the ball can bounce over this barrier. Previously this move was considered to be unsporting. But if a fielder cannot reach the ball otherwise with the hands or any other body-part, a foot, placed sideways, can prove very useful.

HIGH CATCHES

Right positioning is the key-note behind every high catch. If the fielder is able to get into a right position as early as possible, he/she will be able to get ample time to concentrate on the ball that is travelling towards him/her. Needless to say, the actual catch is sure to become a lot easier.

ENGLISH-STYLE CATCHES

In this catch, a fielder looks at the ball when it is at almost shoulder high keeping the head high and also cupping the hands together with fingers spread out. The eyes are on the ball right till the catch has been achieved. The ball should be taken at the base of the fingers, not on their tips. Getting the ball in the hands, the hands must be brought down and a little nearer the chest. It will help the fielder to cushion the ball, catch it and save the hands from the sting of the ball. This done, the fingers should grip the ball and draw it towards the body in order to retain its grip.

AN AUSTRALIAN-TYPE CATCH

This type of catch is made by many fielders on bright sunny days (full of glare). It is also used when the ball is travelling although high, yet along a horizontal path towards them. For this catch, hands are high but slightly to one side of the head and the palms are facing the ball. Watchfully, the ball is grabbed using the cushioning actions. Then the hands, along with the ball, are brought to the shoulder past the ear.

JUDGEMENT PAYS

Whatever the style of the catch, the fielder should judge wisely the track off the ball's flight and estimate where it is going to fall. He/She must not rush in much too far as it can be risky. Moving forwards is always a lot easier than moving backwards watching the ball over the shoulders. As the ball drops down, the fielder should come underneath and grab it.

HIGH-CATCH DRILL

For practising high-catches, it is wise to go to an open area with a friend and a tennis ball. Ask your friend to throw the ball to a very good height and then get into a position under the ball in order to make a catch. Practise all the styles that have been studied. With increased confidence, the tennis ball can be replaced with a cricket ball.

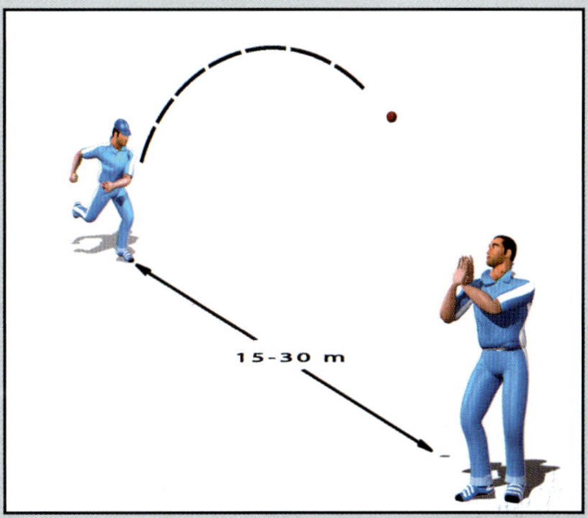

THE BOUNDARY

If any part of the fielder's body crosses the boundary line when he/she is in contact with the ball, the batsman will get a boundary and he/she will not be declared out even if the fielder has made the catch.

But, the fielder can knock the ball back before it touches the boundary line. Then the fielder can run over the boundary before returning to collect the ball.

The fielder knocks the ball back and then steps over the rope.

The fielder must be back inside the rope before picking up the ball.

ATTACKING THE BALL

While fielding near a wicket if the fielder finds the ball coming a bit gently, his/her should swoop on it and throw it quickly over the wicket. It is sure to prevent the batsman from taking a run or even lead to a run-out. The ball can be attacked and picked up by only one hand and thrown immediately.

The fielder should bend his/her knees after getting near the ball. Keeping low, the ball should be scooped into the throwing arm back as soon as possible. Then the ball should be thrown to one end of the pitch. If the wicket is quite close, the fielder may be able to bowl the aim underarm—all in one and the same movement.

RUN-OUTS

A speedy pick-up and accurate instant throw are the key-notes for achieving a run-out. But quick brain is equally essential. In a moment, it should be figured out which end to throw in.

RUN-OUTS CHECK-LIST

1. Which batsman is the farthest from safety?
2. Which end am I (the fielder) the closest to?
3. Which end is the best suited to a throw in?
4. Is there someone to back up the move?

If the fielder can't answer these questions, it is best to throw the ball to the wicket-keeper's end.

RUN-OUT PRACTICE

The best fielder practises achieving run-outs aiming at one stump whatever the distance between his/her and the stump. The fielder must be realistic and aim at something larger to begin with. Run-out skills can be improved on one's own using a tennis ball, a wall and a wicket-sized cardboard box.

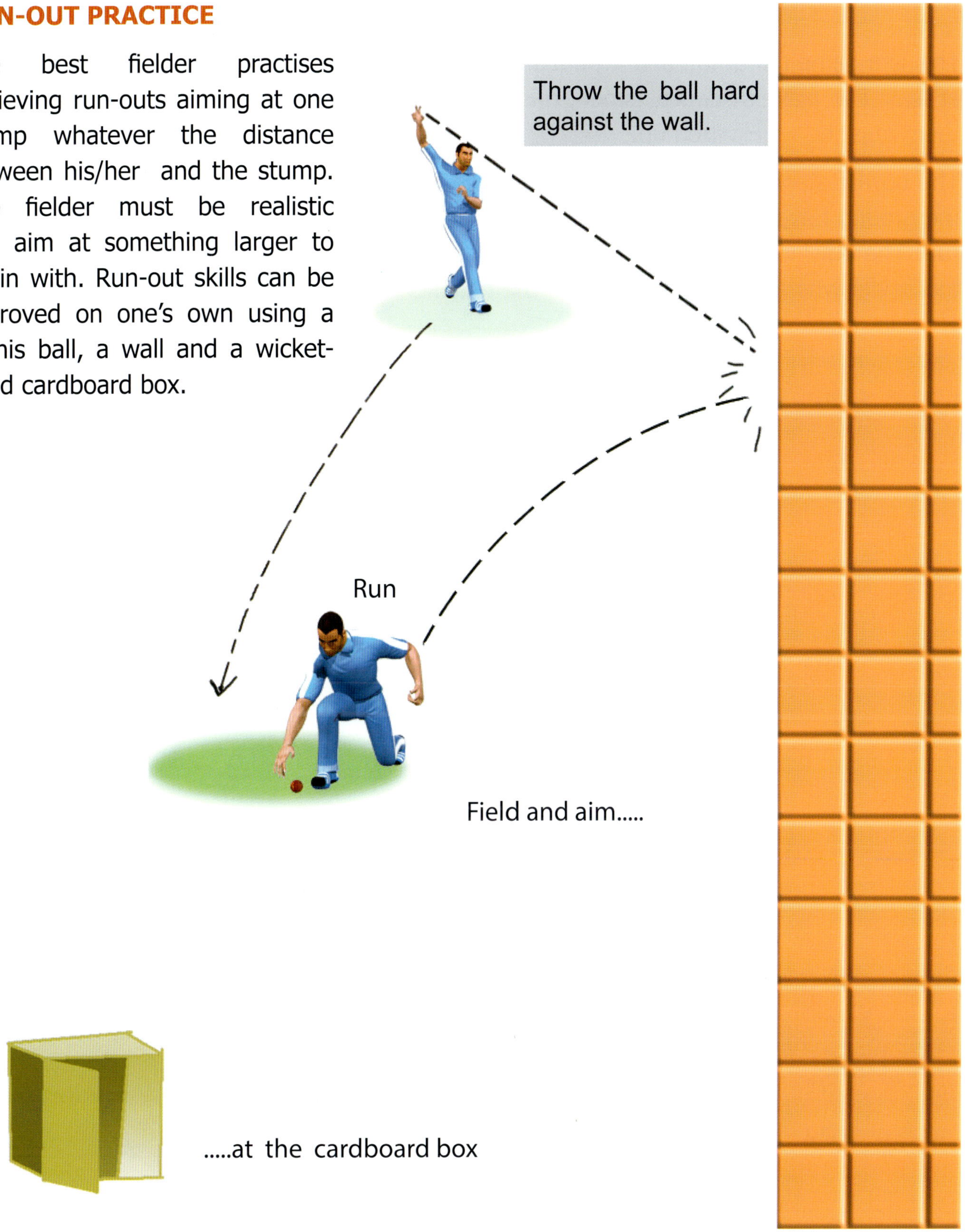

The tennis ball should be thrown hard at the wall. As soon as it returns, it must be collected and thrown at the cardboard box. The ball must be bounced off the wall at an angle to practise throwing it in from various directions.

Under-Pressure Practice

This is a game full of fun and it puts pressure on the close fielders and batsmen. It needs at least five players—two batsmen, one fielder, one bowler and one wicket-keeper. All of them must be well knitted up.

The bowler stands one-third of the way down the pitch and he throws the ball hard along the ground towards the fielder. As soon as the ball is released the batsmen tries to take a run. The bowler and the wicket-keeper get behind the wickets to recover the throw from the fielder who aims at getting one of the batsmen out.

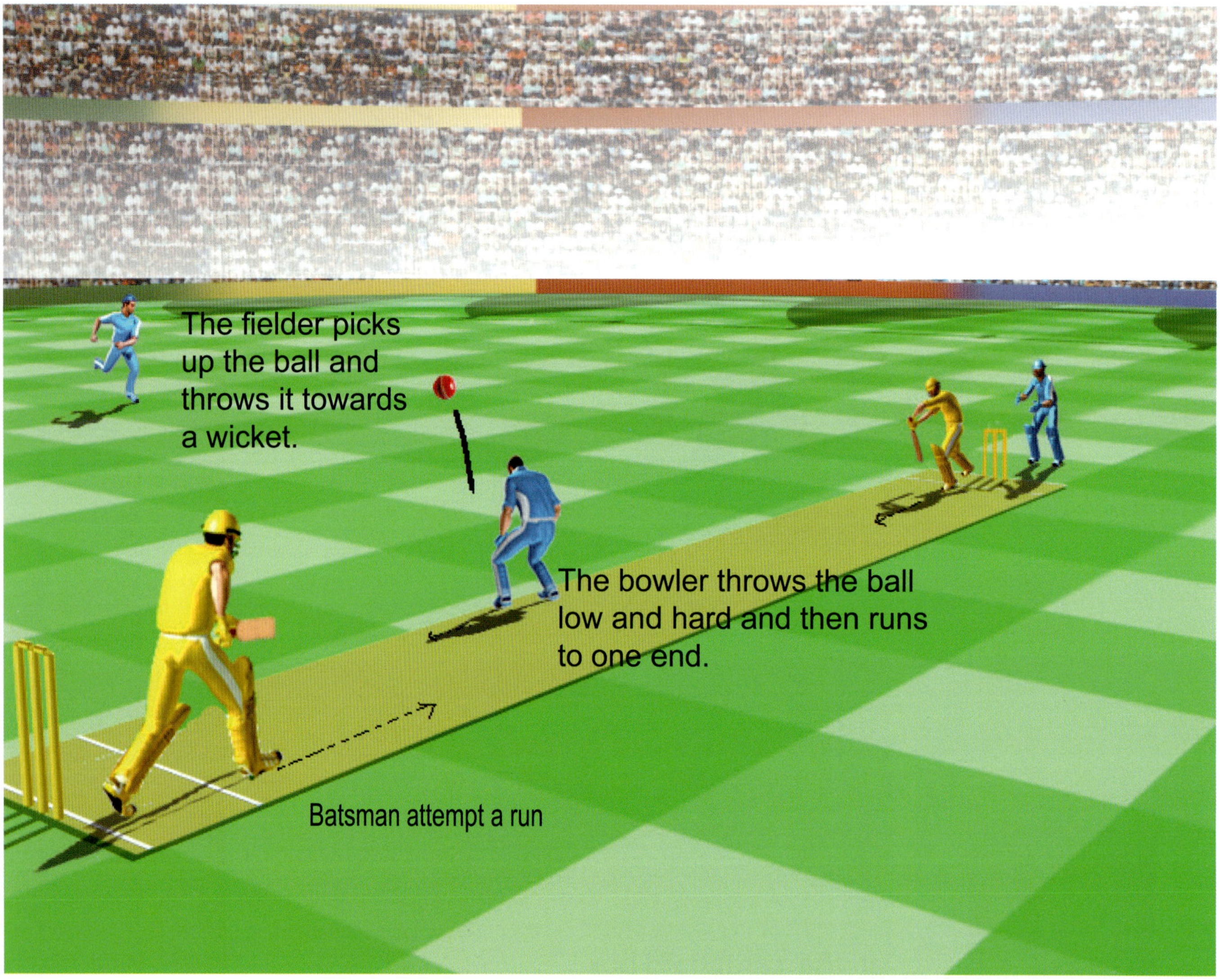

WHOOPS !
If the fielder drops a catch or misfields a ball, he/she must not feel disappointed. It can happen to any player—even the best one. This lapse should be brushed aside followed by concentration on fielding the next ball.

CLOSE CATCHES

BASIC CLOSE CATCH

The fielder should stand crouched with knees bent, eyes level, feet shoulder-width or a bit more apart and the body-weight on the balls of the feet. The hands should the cupped in front with palms just touching each other from inside. The finger-ends must not be sticked out as it can cause them to be hurt.

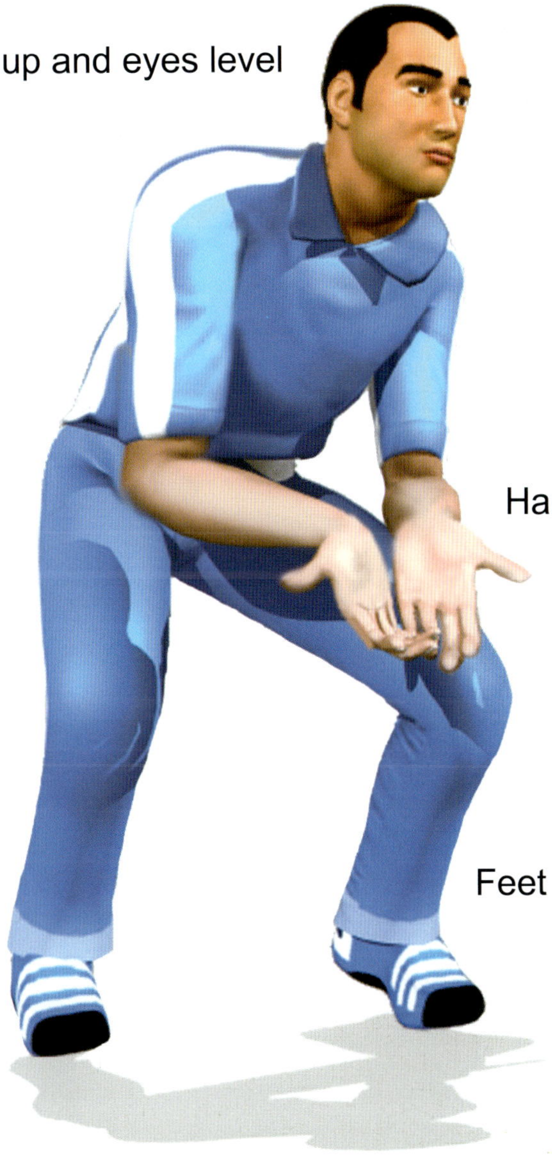

The advantage of this position is that the fielder is ready for all types of catching opportunities—a diving catch to one side; an upward spring to catch a high ball and a forward lounge for a short catch—if the fielder's body and mind should be ready for these. Staying alert and concentrating on the ball as soon as it leaves the bowler's hand are the key-notes of all the types of good close catches.

CALLING

If the fielder is confident of his best position to field or catch a ball, he/she must call out to his team-mates clearly and loudly about it so that no team-mate may get into his or her way to interrupt the attempt by bumping into the fielder. When the ball is skied near the wicket, the wicket-keeper, with his gloves and catching expertise, must call for the catch.

PRACTISING CLOSE-CATCHES

For an exciting game of close-catching the fielders must form a cordon around a thrower keeping about 10-15 metres away from him/her. The thrower should spin around and then throw the ball from below the shoulder flatly towards one of the fielders. It needs good reactions and hands.

For slip fielding, the fielders must make a cordon only 8-10 metres away from the thrower who should throw the ball from below waist-height.

DIVING CATCHES

The fielder may be a natural diver or not. Practice for dives should be done on something soft to land on.

DIVING IN ALL DIRECTIONS

Beginners often believe that trying for a diving catch is purely a matter of leaping to one side or the other. No, it is no so. The fielder may have to leap forwards because many catching chances off the bat drop just short of close fielders. So while fielding in the slips or at gully, the fielder must work in forward-diving skills as well.

Chapter Six

Developing Your Batting

Of all cricket's skill, batting is the most glamorous. In this chapter we shall study a few selected and more advanced batting strokes. Though batting is a very vast subject, the batsman who masters these advanced strokes along with the shots gone through in chapter 3, he/she will be well on the way to refined batting.

VARIOUS DRIVES

Drives are high-quality run-scoring strokes made mainly off the front foot. They can be played to over-pitched deliveries and half-vollyes.

With the back foot in position, the batsman can move his/her front foot in an arc on both sides of the wicket. Whatever type of drive is played, the front foot needs to get close to the pitch of the ball ; but not so close that there isn't any room for the batsman's hands to swing through.

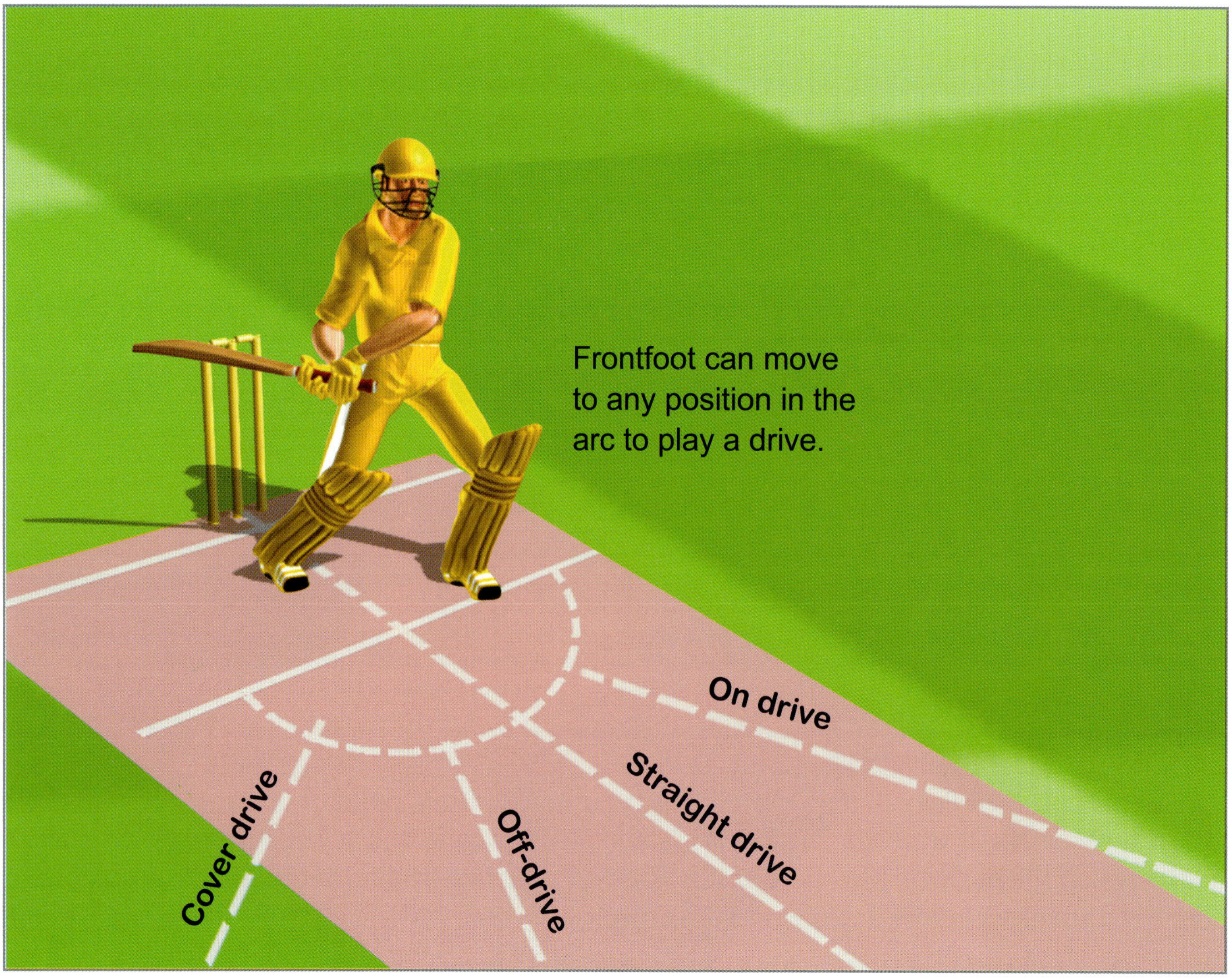

THE OFF-DRIVE

This drive is played to a half-volley around or just outside the off-stump.

As the batsman moves his/her feet into position, he/she points the shoulders straight at the ball. The turn of the shoulders lends power to the shot. A drive is a swing, not a punch or push.

As the batsman hits the ball, his/her top arm should be really straight, head down and hands over the ball. The body-weight should be entirely on the front foot.

The hands are allowed to lead the bat into the follow-through which can be full or a checked one. But a full follow-through always requires the batsman to bend his/her wrists.

Towards the finish of the follow through, the rear shoulder moves under the chin. The batsman must aim at finishing the stroke with the bottom arm almost or completely extended.

THE COVER DRIVE

This drive is very similar to an off-drive except that it is played to a ball that has been bowled a bit wider. The drive dispatches the ball to the outfield through the covers. In order to perform this drive, shoulders need to be turned firmly and fairly more.

A cover drive

THE ON-DRIVE

This drive is usually played to a ball heading for leg-stump and it involves a much harder shot than those for any other drive. Many players believe that they have to be over-balance towards the off-side while making the shot. It can be well-checked by dipping the head and the front shoulder while moving in for the stroke.

> The front leg must be placed outside the line of the ball.

THE LOFTED DRIVE

This drive is a well-calculated attacking attempt that is played to slow or medium-pace deliveries. It involves a powerful hit over the heads of the fielders into the open space behind them. The ball is hit just short of a half-volley. While playing this drive, a batsman—

(a) must keep the head down and not lift it too soon.

(b) must not lean back while playing the stroke.

(c) must play a full drive giving it some oomph.

(d) must aim at a high follow-through.

DRIVING DRILL

Given below is quality drive drill for a small group of players. One player bowls underarm so that the ball may bounce on a small spot in front of the batsman's off-stump. The batsman looks to drive the ball towards one of the fielders positioned on the off-side.

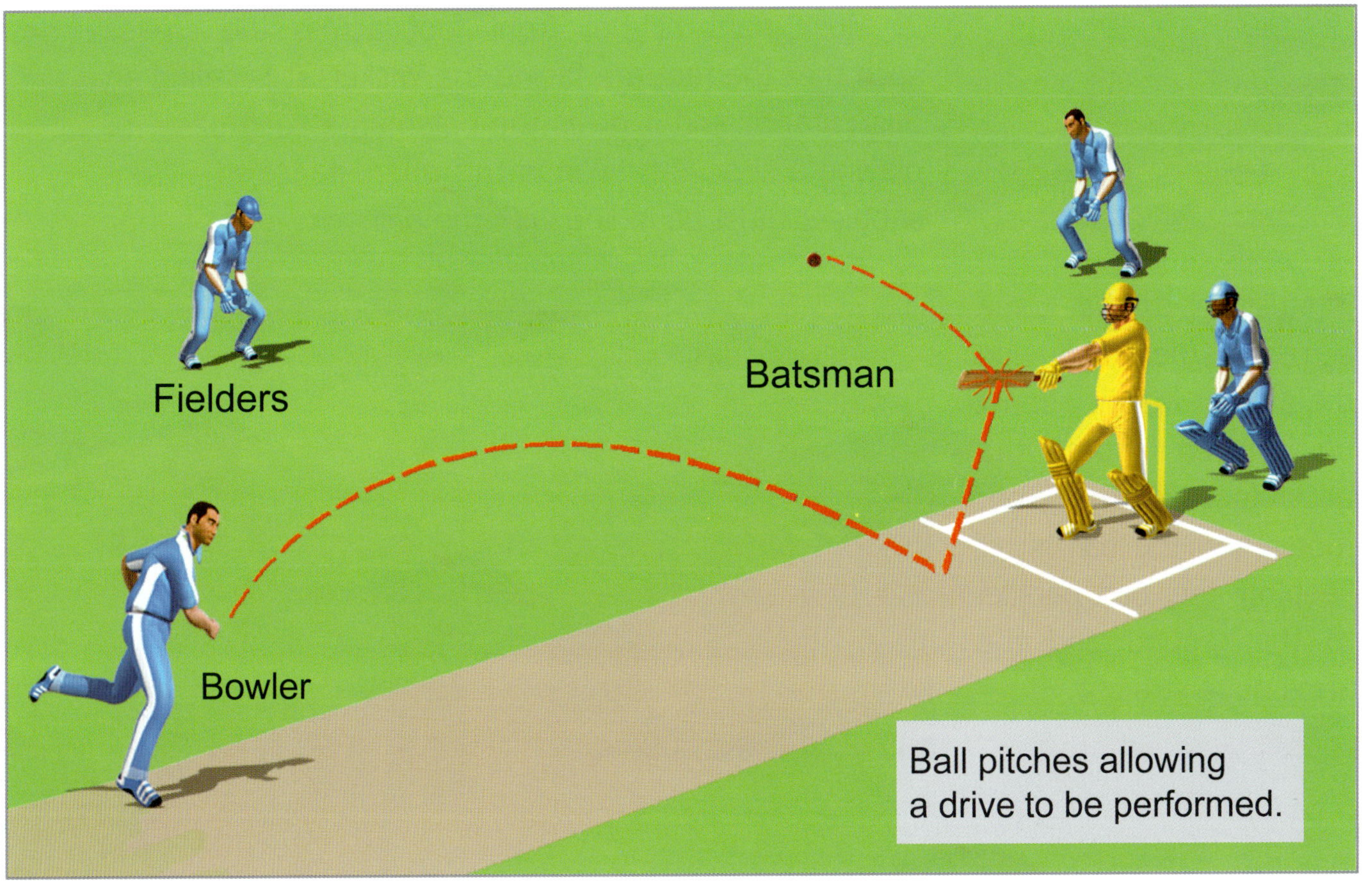

If there is a particular difficulty while turning your drive stroke, the bowler should be asked to bowl the ball such that it arrives in a position suited to a drive after its second bounce.

PULLS AND CUTS

THE PULL

The pull can be best played against a ball that is heading just wide of the leg-stump or is short and pitching on leg-stump. For a pull, a batsman—

1. Must step back and get his/her back foot across the wickets with the toes, pointing down the wicket. While performing this, the shoulder must be kept in line with the ball.

2. Must plant his/her front foot across the crease such that the feet are facing the wicket. It is called an open stance and it gives the batsman a solid base for playing a shot. But even in this open stance, the front shoulder must be in line with the ball.

3. Must let the bat come across his/her body and the body-weight must be moved from the back foot to the front foot. Then the ball is hit keeping the bat parallel to the ground and the arms quite straight.

4. Must while hitting, work his/her bottom hand so that it may bring the bat around for a follow-through keeping the hand still as long as possible.

BALANCE

Balance is highly important for a batsmen. Many batsman, including greats like Ian Botham, lost their balance while playing pull-shots and hook-shots and fell on the wicket. So practice of shots must be done with stumps in place but not using a ball. It will help the practiser get used to keeping the body in balance while swivelling around.

THE SQUARE CUT

This cut is played to a ball that is wide of the off-stump. It is indeed a very exciting powerful stroke but needs one precaution. It must not be attempted when the ball is too close to the body as it often leads to an unhappy dismissal.

For a square cut, the back foot should be moved across the stumps roughly pointing to where the batsman intends the ball to go. The back knee must be but enough so that, as the bat is brought around, it may be parallel to the ground. The arms should be stretched while hitting the ball and the entire body-weight must be on the back foot.

The wrists should be rolled to keep the ball down and during the follow-through, the back shoulder should move under the chin.

GLANCES AND SWEEPS

These two types of shots require less power but a lot of timing. Only a couple of very common strokes are studied below in this range.

THE BACK FOOT LEG-GLANCE

This delicate shot can get a batsman plenty of runs especially when there is no leg-side fielder such as a leg-slip in attendance. The batsman has to pick the ball wisely and delicately just missing the leg-stump.

The shot must be played close to the body but making sure a reasonable contact between the bat and the ball. Bear in mind that if the batsman stretches the bat to reach the ball and catches it too fine, there is a big chance for the wicket-keeper or a close fielder to make a catch.

THE SWEEP

A sweep is a risky attacking shot that is played against a spin bowler who has bowled a delivery well up and outside the batsman's leg-stump. This shot is made in a crouching position with the ball hit almost on the half volley.

As the ball approaches, the batsman should put his front foot down the wicket in order to meet the ball in a way just similar to that used in the start of a forward defensive stroke. The front leg must be bent fully and the back leg should trail such that the back knee touches or almost touches the ground.

The ball is hit just after it has pitched but before it has bounced up. The wrists are rolled a little to keep the ball down as it is hit into the area behind square leg.

The reader must have seen a reverse sweep being played on TV. But it must be avoided as it is far too risky and very few of the great batsman ever bother with it.

A reverse sweep

THE HIGH-RISK SHOTS

It is wise to practise this shot on the nets only and not in a real match until at batsman is really on top of his/her batting. If played well, these shots can score a lot of runs. But they are much too risky.

THE LATE CUT

It is a tricky shot that despatches the ball wide of the slips in test matches but, in one-day games, through the actual slip area. In it, the bat is controlled by the wrists keeping the hands well about the height of the ball. The ball is stroked down gently making a very late contact when it goes past the batsman.

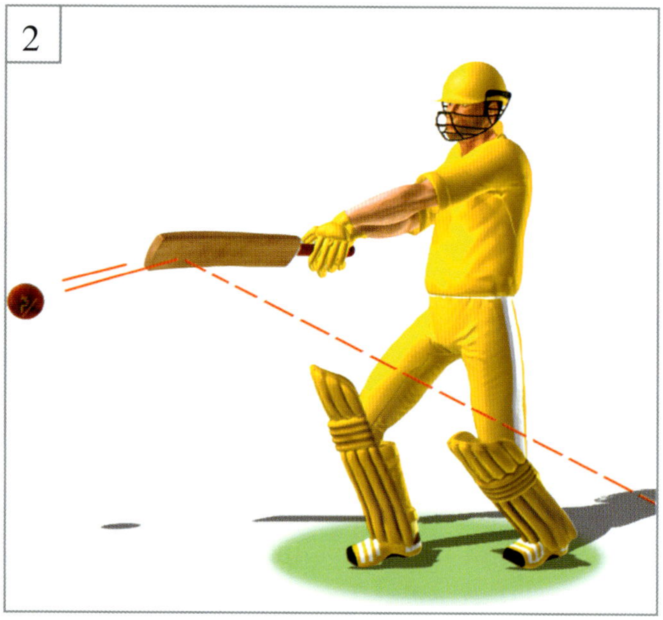

THE HOOK

It is one of the best shots when the batsman is in top form and has a helmet on. It is played to a short-pitched delivery reaching the batsman at about chest height and needing a very quick reaction.

The batsman must get his/her weight on the back foot that should be moving back and across the stumps. While moving the body to meet the ball, the hands must be kept high and the arms straight as well as parallel to the ground. While making contact with the ball, the batsman must swivel on the feet keeping the arms straight. Wrists must be rolled in order to angle the bat's face for keeping the ball down.

For practising this stroke, a few robust friends and a tennis ball should be used. They should throw the ball strongly and the batsman must concentrate on the stroke. The batsman must not mind giving chances for catches during early practice.

RABBITS AND FERRETS

These two terms are used for lower-order batsmen, i.e. tail-enders. A rabbit is a player who is scared of batting while a ferret is even worse. Ferrets come in for play after the rabbits.

Chapter Seven

Developing Your Bowling

A consistent line and length of each bowled delivery is the key-note of good bowling (see page 51). It should be mastered well enough before practising bowling. A medium-paced bowler must bowl his/her basic ball on a good length with a line on or around the off-stump. Bowling in a highly accurate line and length is a successful wicket-taking weapon by itself only if the bowler bowls in the right spot ball after ball. Though this weapon is often under estimated.

WHAT IS A GOOD LENGTH ?

A delivery bowled at good length makes the batsman unsure whether to go forwards or backwards. And when a good length is combined with bowling line, the batsman becomes uncertain whether he can leave the ball or has to play it. Such a bowling creates for the bowler a good target area which is referred to as the corridor of uncertainty by commentators.

VARIATIONS IN LINE AND LENGTH

Variation in the line and length of bowling deliveries can prove very useful indeed. A bowler may choose to bowl straight at the stumps if the batsman looks nervous and poor. But for a tall competent batsman used to playing forward, the basic deliveries can be shortened a little.

Control of line and length is vital for a good bowler. A yorker when the ball pitches around the popping crease and goes underneath the bat, is a great delivery. But if it is short, it becomes a half volley which allows the batsman to score runs.

BOWLING TIGHT

Whatever the type of a bowler, it is not desirable to bowl five decent deliveries and then bowl a bad one. In this way the pressure built on the batsman by the decent five deliveries gets relieved instantly and he/she can despatch a full toss or even long hop for four runs. Bowling maiden overs as far as possible should be aimed at.

PACE ACE

Some fast bowlers rely purely on their frightening pace (speed) : 130—140 km/h for test match "quicks" and bouncers to take wickets. This happens, however, very rarely as a dead pitch often limits their effectiveness. Most pace bowlers endeavour to add swing or seam or lethal slower delivery (see page 90) and bouncers to their weapons as well as pure speed.

THE BOUNCER

A bouncer is a short-pitched delivery rearing up at the batsman forcing him to play a hasty shot or go in for an evasive action. A bouncer well wide of the batsman or going over his/her head is a wasted delivery. These words do not aim at preventing a bowler from trying bouncers. But it is forcefully suggested that bouncers should be played at the nets or against a genuine batsman wearing a helmet and other full protective gear.

MOVEMENT

Unpredictably movement is an effective weapon of a bowler. Fast and medium pace bowlers endeavour to move the ball through the air (swing) or off the pitch (seam). Some of them are capable of performing both these movements.

SEAM BOWLING

Seam bowling means making the ball land vertically on the seam and letting the pitch deviate the ball one way or the other. For it, the bowler must use the basic group (see chapter 4) keeping the wrist loose enough to flick the ball down while releasing it. The flick gives the ball some backward spin helping it to stay on the seam and holding the pitch while landing. Seam bowling is best suited to a green pitch—one that is damp and has a lot of grass on it to let the ball grip it and then deviate from it. Out and out seam bowlers are generally fast bowlers who rely on speed and variations in their pace. Alternately, they may be really accurate fast-medium pacers.

Bowling is, in fact, a pretty tiring job. So it is to advisable go in for the following questions after a session on the nets. The answers to some of the questions are very surprising and make good ordinary facts to be shared by the bowler with his or her friends.

1. What is the maximum score off a ball in a modern game?
2. What are the best figures recorded by a bowler in a first-class innings?
3. Who holds the record as the fastest bowler and how fast?
4. Who has taken the most wickets in test matches?
5. What feat did Jim Laker achieve for England against Australia in 1956?

Answers to the above questions are

1. 17 by Gary Champman for Banyule Cricket against Macleod in Australia in 1990. There were no overthrows. The runs were made on the ball disappeared in 25 cm highgrass on the pitch.
2. 10 Wickets for 10 runs, by Hedley Verity for Yorkshire against Nottinhamshire in 1930.
3. Australian Jeff Thomson whose fastest delivery was timed at 160.5 km/h.
4. At the time of writing, Sri Lanka spinner Muttiah Muralitharan has taken 800 wickets in 133 test Matches.
5. Amazing bowling figures over the two innings of 19 for 90.

SWINGS

Swing means the movement of the ball in mid-air due to atmospheric condition—wind, direction of the seam's face and the polish on the ball. Thus scientific factors are also involved in a swing. Yet the bottom line depends on a lot of practice. With one side of the ball towards the batsman or away from him/her. And this capability to swing the ball is a very useful bowling weapon.

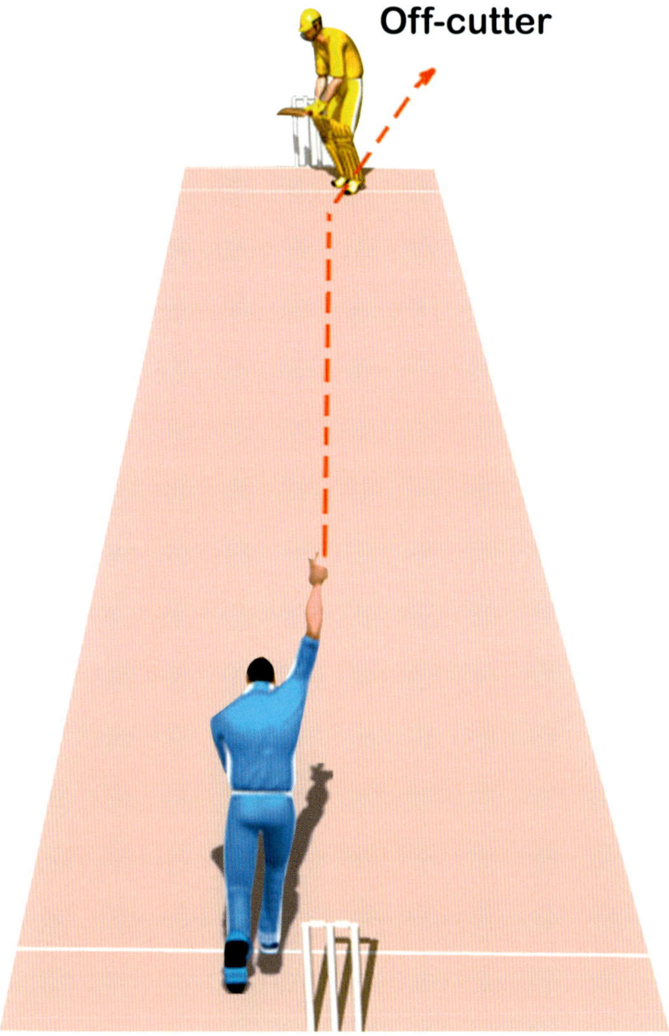

Whether it is an in-swinger or an out-swinger, the bowler's action must be similar to the basic action described in chapter 4. Still his/her fingers must be behind the ball while the wrist should be firm. It is equally important that the bowler's arm is high and a strong follow-through is there. Swing deliveries need to be well-pitched up so that they may get more time to swing in the air and dodge the batsman.

THE IN-SWINGER

One modification in the bowler's action can help him or her bowl better in-swingers. The bowler should try to be a little less to the on-side than usual placing the front foot a bit to the off-side while taking the delivery stride.

THE OUT-SWINGER

It is a deadly move and accounts for more wickets than any other delivery in cricket. It is best bowled from close to the stumps and, unlike the in-swinger, with the body kept to the on-side as long as possible.

PRACTISING SWINGS

For excellent practice one must bowl in-swingers and out-swingers on a spare pitch with a wicket-keeper at the other end.

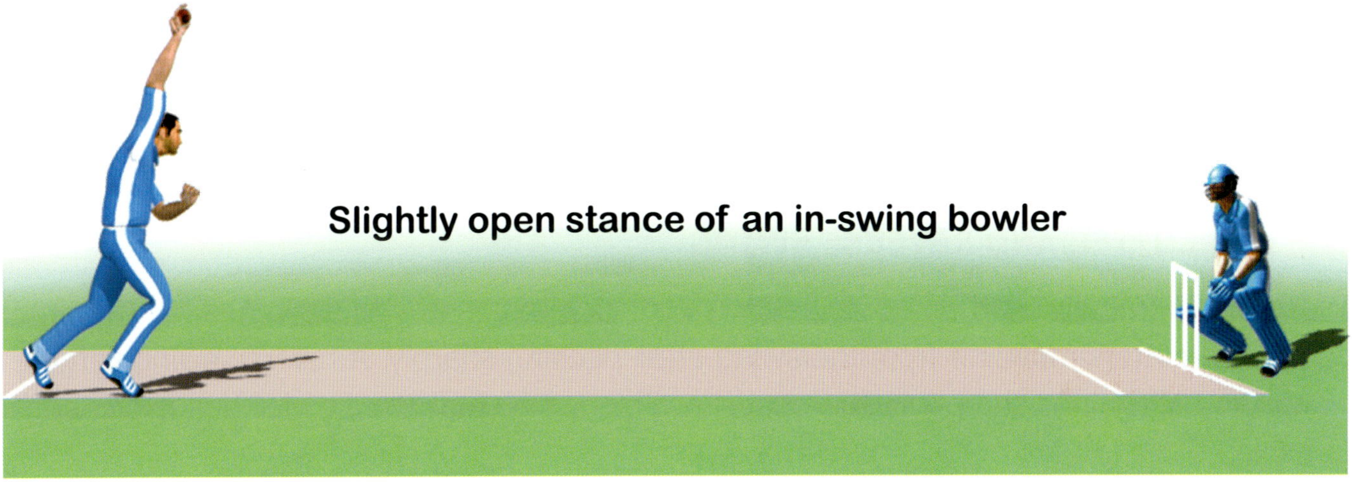

THE OFF-CUTTER

An off-cutter is closely related to the out-swinger and it is pitched up around the off-stump just like the out-swinger. But in it, the ball moves towards the leg-side after it has pitched. It works best on a dry or dusty pitch. A bowler who can bowl off-cutter and out-swinger is sure to put the batsman into grave trouble, in fact.

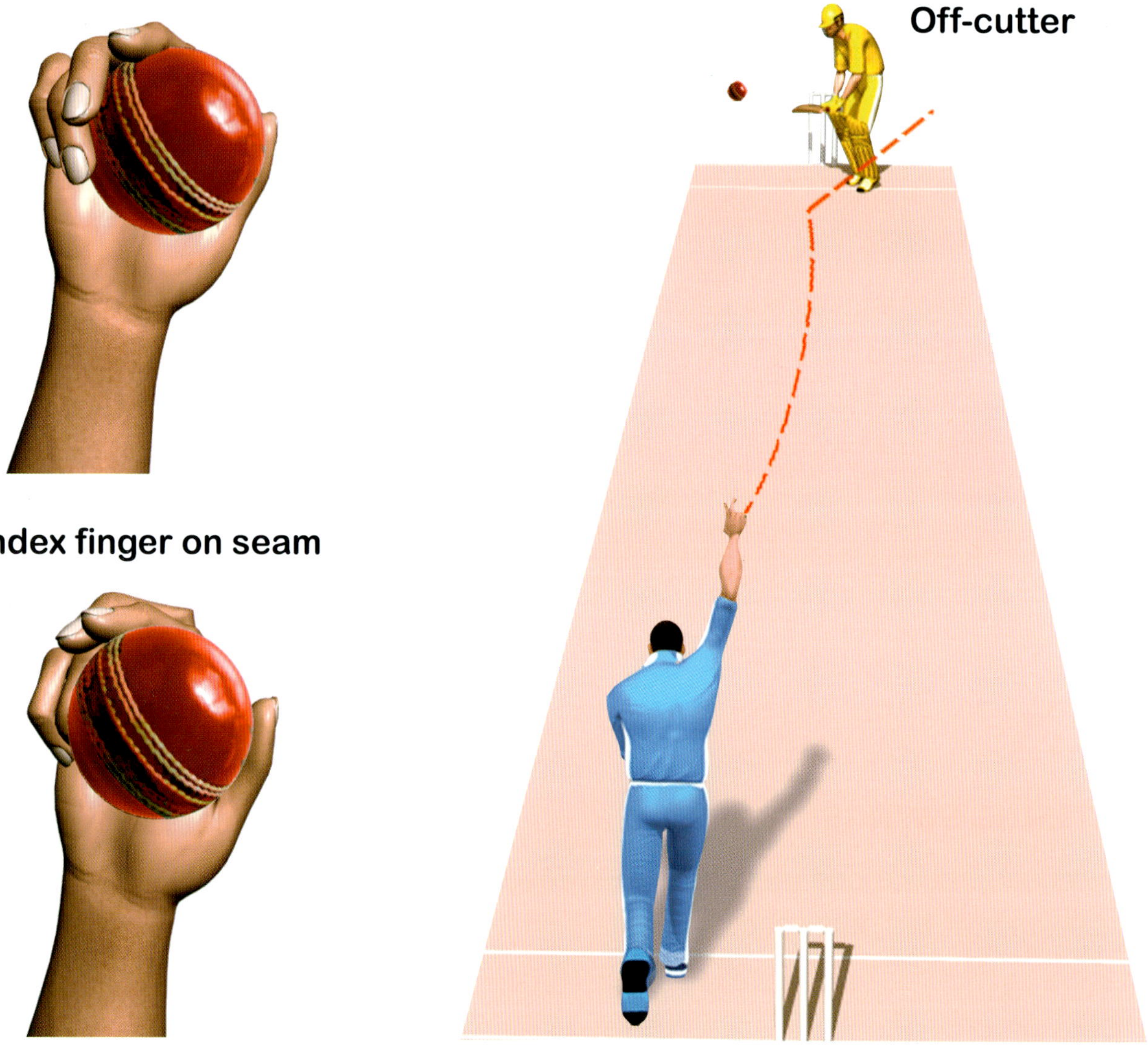

While releasing the ball, the bowler should drag his/her first two fingers across the ball with the first finger pulling the seam down clock-wise.

THE LEG-CUTTER AND REVERSE SWING

These are extremely hard to bowl. It is wise to stick to the easier deliveries for the time being. Leg-cutters move off from the swing after pitching sharply. A reverse swing is there when the ball swings sharply in the opposite direction to that the bowler has expected it to move.

SPIN BOWLING

Spin bowling or slow bowling is a perfect art worthy of a complete book on itself alone. Spinners are often as much mistreated by their own captains as by the opposing batsmen. But on right types of pitch, they win matches regularly. To be a spinner, a bowler needs top match temperament. He/She needs to forget about the previous ball which, being poor, may have been hit for six runs. His/Her full concentration should be on the next ball.

The wrist and the fingers twist while making the delivery

TIPS FOR SPIN BOWLING

1. A spinner needs to bring about a wide variety in his/her deliveries to keep the bats man guessing. This variety can be achieved through speed and the flight of each delivery.
2. A spinner must keep practising spin-bowling whenever and as much as he/she can. As for line and length, they can be worked on the nets.
3. The practiser should carry a rubber ball with him and use it to strengthen his/her fingers and the wrist.

THE OFF-SPINNER

Off-spinner are often called finger-spinners because it is the first finger of the spin-bowler that has to do most of the spinning work. An off-spinner's basic delivery to a right-handed batsman pitches on the off-side and turns to the leg-side, i.e. into the batsman. Let us observe the all-important grip.

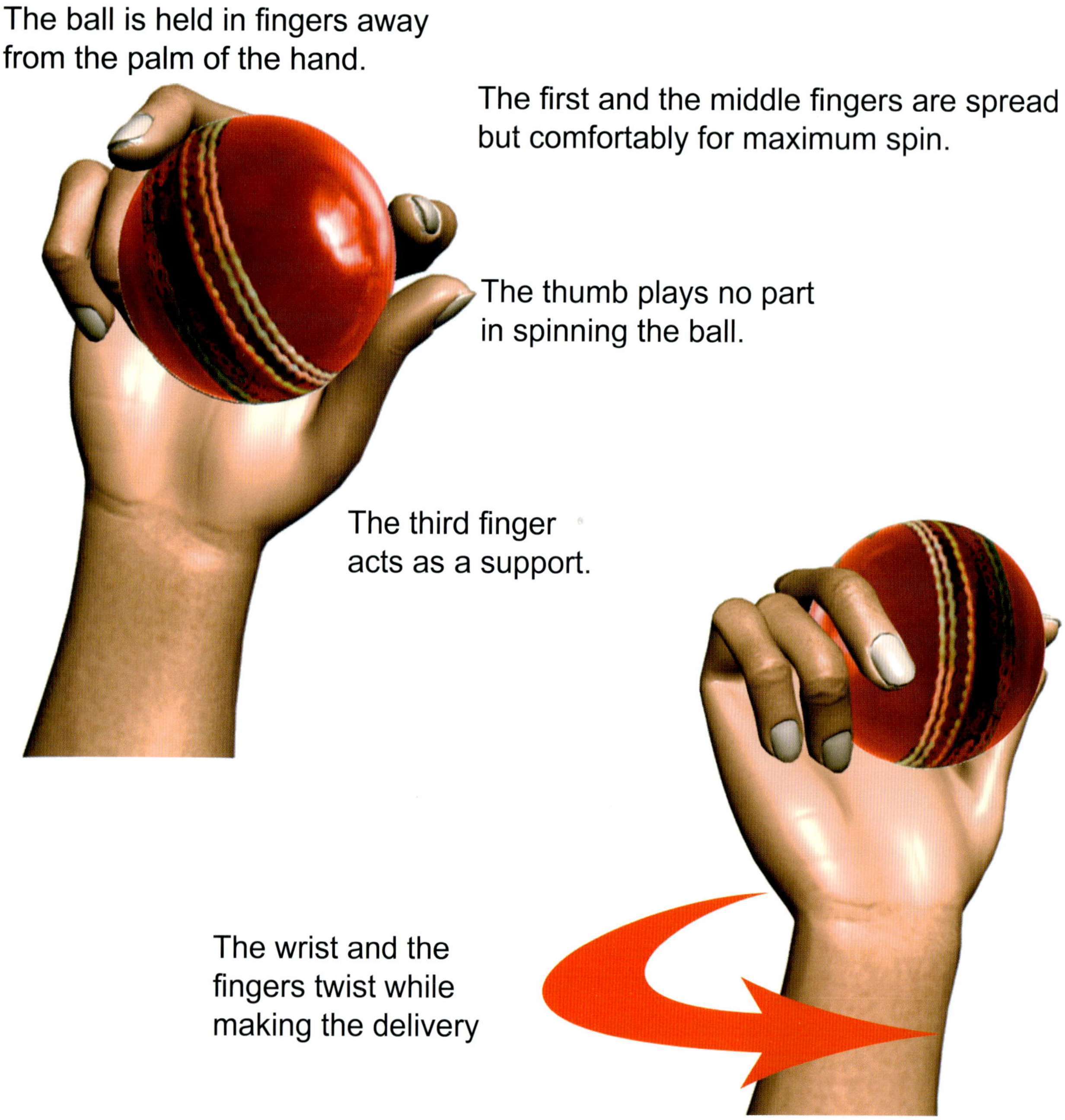

ACTION

The action is similar to the basic action stated in chapter 4. But the bowler's rear leg should be slightly across the crease and the front leg must be braced. With the palm of the hand facing up, the wrist and the fingers should be twisted sharply clockwise till the ball has left the hand.

RELEASE

Another way of thinking about the release is to imagine opening a stiff ball-sized round door-handle above the head. The bowler must think of the strong tweak that he/she will have to give that handle in order to open the door. It is just similar to the required spinning action.

The bowler must experiment with his / her grip. Different grips may be required to be successful on different pitches.

LEFT-ARM OFF-SPINNER

The bowler should adopt the same grip and action as a right-handed off-spinner would do. But the left-handed bowler is more likely to bowl from around the wicket. He/She can pose different problems to most of the right-handed batsmen by moving the ball away rather than into the batsman.

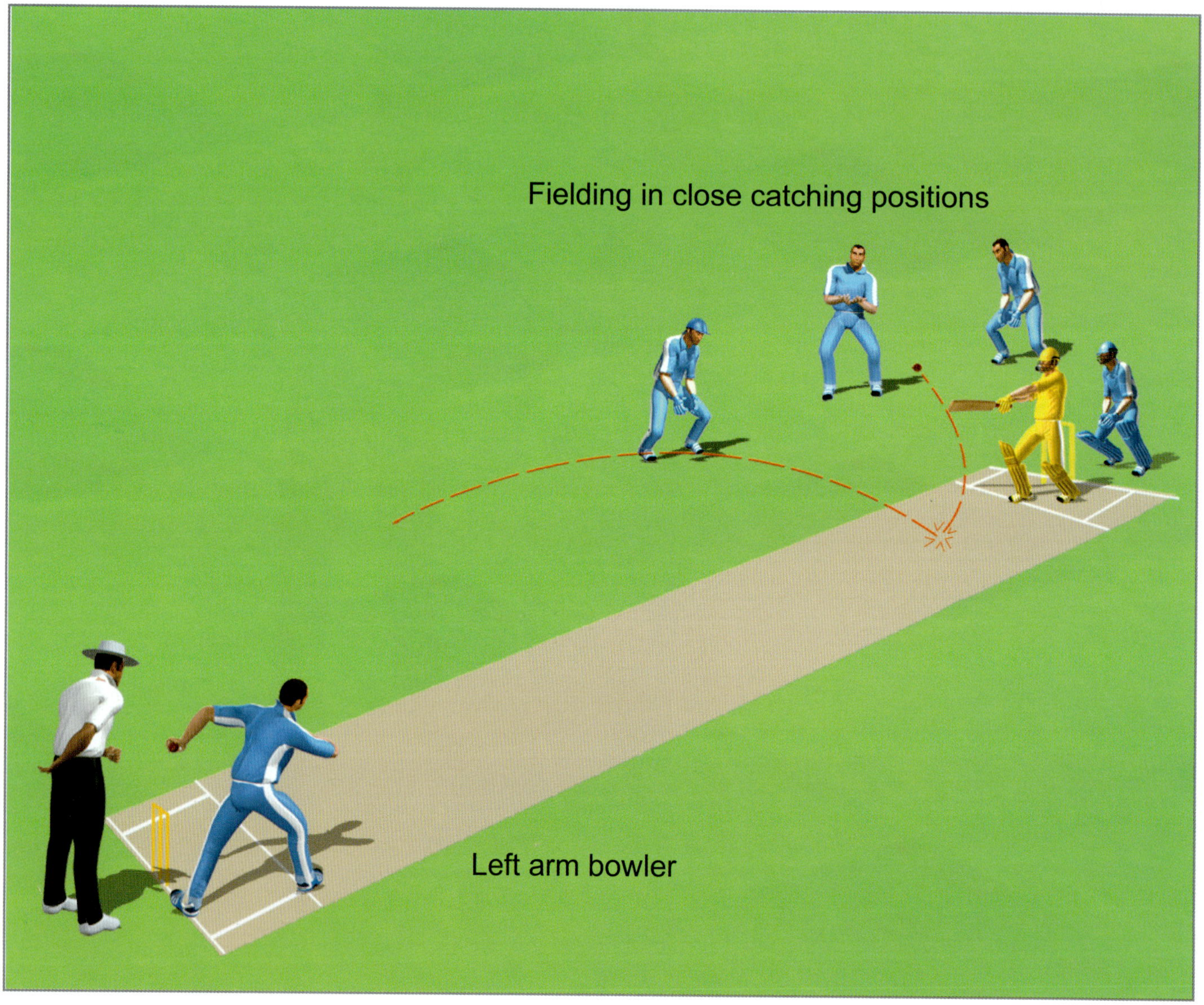

THE LEG-SPINNER

No book on the game of cricket will ever be complete without making a mention of the leg-spin. It is a type of spin-bowling in which the ball moves from the leg-side to the off-side after it has pitched. The delivery involves a strong wrist action. The leg-spin is becoming increasingly popular again since the advent of brilliant players like Abdul Qadir and Shane Warne.

WRIST WORK

Leg-spinners may be referred to as wrist-spinners because it is the wrist that they use to spin the ball. A leg-spinner's bowling action is just similar to that of an off-spinner, i.e. side on and slightly across the crease. The only difference between the two is in what is done with the arm-end. A leg-spinner's wrist is bent dragging the seam anti-clock wise.

The third finger drags around
the bottom-half of the seam

The seam lies
crosswise

The thumb-
base acts
as a support

The ball held quite firmly.

The wrist turns on delivery so
that............

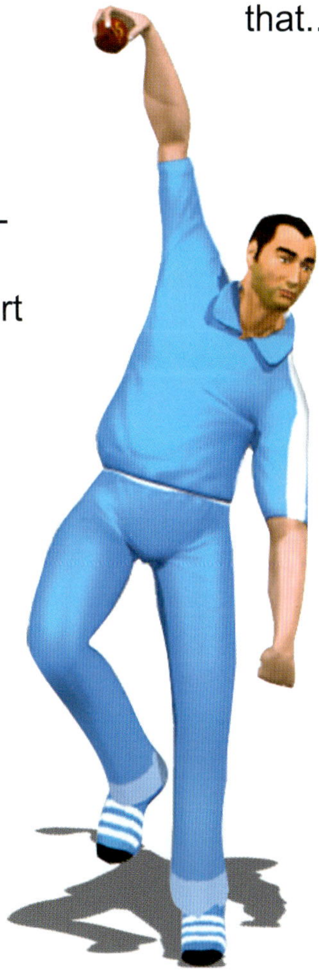

the back of the hand,
is towards the batsman
just after delivery

Bowling a leg-spinner

THE GOOGLY

The googly or "Wrong 'un" is a very difficult ball for the batsman. The bowler's grip is the same as that for the leg-break. But the bowler points his/her wrist towards the batsman while releasing the ball. The ball, then, becomes an off-spinner moving from the off-side to the leg-side.

VARYING THE DELIVERY

A bowler keeps, varying his/her deliveries. It can keep a batsman guessing and push him/her into uncertainty. For a fast bowler, a much slower delivery disguised by a normal looking action, can really puzzle a batsman who may have been adjusted to the bowler's pace.

Similarly, an arm ball—a faster delivery—pushed through straight and speedily from a slow bowler can surprise a batsman who is concentrating on the pitch and the spin of the ball.

THE FLIGHTED DELIVERY

Flighting a delivery means pushing the ball up so that it flies higher than usual—particularly one from a slow bowler. With spin, a flighted ball suddenly dips before pitching. Commentators often describe it saying, "The bowler has given the ball some air."

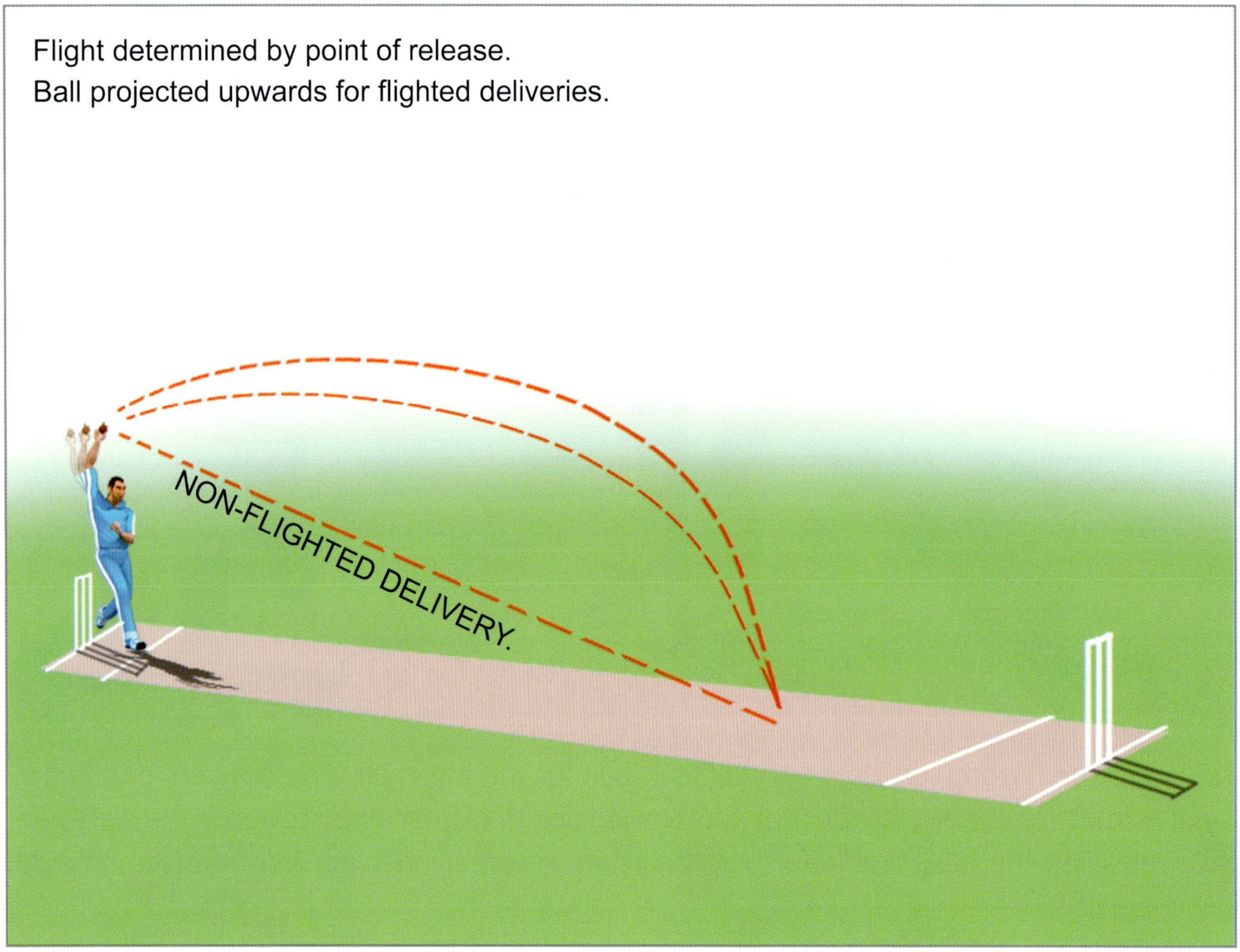

VARYING THE ANGLE

Altering the angle at which a delivery travels to the batsman is another handy bowling tactic. A bowler can use full middle of the crease or can bowl both around or over the wicket. But he/she must tell the umpire from which side to bowl.

1. Balls are bowled wide of the crease over the wicket for yorkers and bouncers.
2. Balls are bowled over the wicket to spear the balls into a right-handed batsman.
3. Balls are bowled around the wicket to slant the balls across a right- handed batsman.

A REAL BATTLE

As a bowler, there is no greater fun in cricket than having a real battle against a batsman. Not only has the bowler to vary his/her deliveries but also to think him out by focusing on him and on how he is playing. Having spotted any weakness, it has to be attacked through bowling.

VITAL STATISTICS

Lovers of cricket love to adore statistics. Batting and bowling figures and averages are keenly observed by spectaculars and commentators alike. To make accurate figures possible, the details of every ball are noted by the official scorer who usually completes end-of-innings cards.

WORLD ELEVEN TEAM

Sachin Tendulkar	b. Lasith Malinga	112
Ricky Ponting	c. Rahul Dravid b. Zaheer Khan	72
Sanath Jayasuriya	c. Mark Boucher b. Harbhajan Singh	40
Brian Lara	Run out	57
Chris Gayle	Stumped Adam Gilchrist	27
Shahid Afridi	lbw. Kieron Pollard	11
M. S. Dhoni	c. Jacques Kallis b. Lasith Malinga	63
Alastair Cook	lbw. Kieron Pollard	24
Muttiah Muralitharan	Run out	11
Anil Kumble	c. AB de Villiers b. Lasith Malinga	8
Shane Warne	b. Kieron Pollard	3
	Extras	16
		444

Do you know what Timed Out stands for?
If a player does not come on the field within two minutes of the previous batter's dismissal, the player can be Timed Out.

BOWLING				
	O	M	R	W
Lasith Malinga	20	4	78	3
Kieron Pollard	20	3	62	2
Zaheer Khan	16	1	76	1
Glenn McGrath	18	3	80	1
Harbhajan Singh	16	0	132	1
Note: O – Over, M – Maidens (over in which no runs are scored), R – Runs Given, W – Wickets taken				

AVERAGES

A bowler's average is given by the number of the runs scored off his/her bowling divided by the number of wickets he/she has taken.

A batsman's average is given by the number of runs he/she has scored divided by the number of times he was out. The greatest batsman of all was Australia's Donald Bradman. who had a test match average of 99.94. How amazing !

A player must not fret over his/her figures or average because they don't always tell the entire story—how after all ?

For example, a bowler bowls very tightly, but does not get a wicket or how a batsman scored only a few runs in extremely tough conditions.

Chapter Eight

Wicket Keeping

A wicket-keeper's position is highly specialised just like that of the goal-keeper in football and it is liable to a lot of comments and jokes. Still it involves a vital job. No other fielder handles the ball as often as the wicket-keeper. Nor does he/she get as many opportunities to stop runs and get the batsmen out. A good wicket-keeper requires deep concentration, a lot of agility and maximum fitness that may make his team-mates emulate him/her.

A wicket-keeper is right in the game all the time. He is in a great position to go up the team, encourage his team-mates and to advise the bowler, if need be. Evidently, he/she must be fit enough to be able to stretch his body really and it needs practice before the game.

Fielder

KEEPER'S KIT

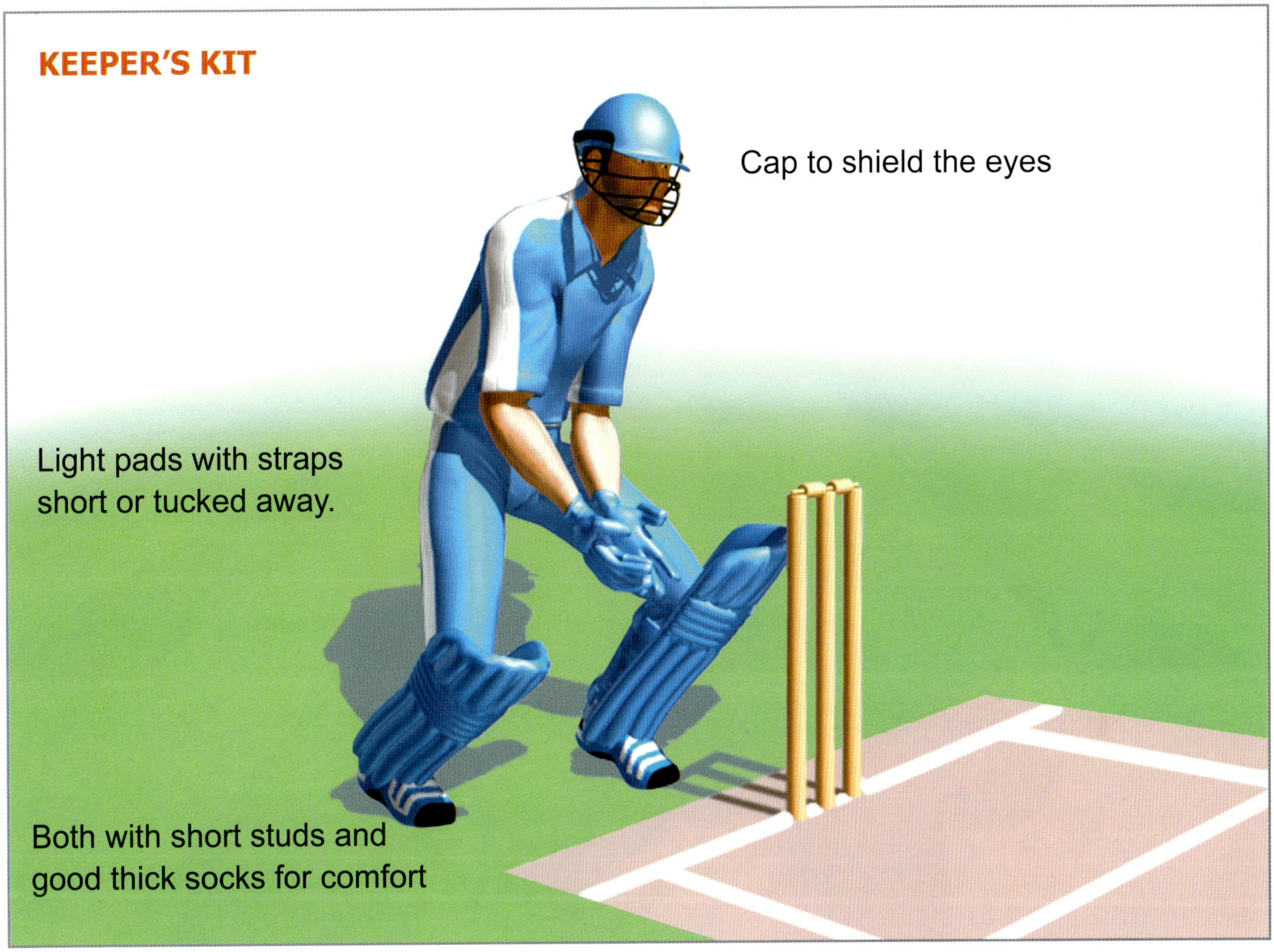

Thin gloves called inners

Main gloves

ABOUT GLOVES

Gloves are the key item in a wicket-keepers's kit. They must be soft and supple as well as large enough to be pulled off in a hurry. The palms of the gloves have rubber dimples which must be replaced, when worn out. Over all, the gloves should be comfortable having enough padding to take out the sting of a fast delivery—but not to the extent that the keeper cannot feel the ball.

STANCE

Stance means everything that makes a wicket-keeper acquire a comfortable position from which he/she can move with speed in all directions. It enables him/her to be half-way there.

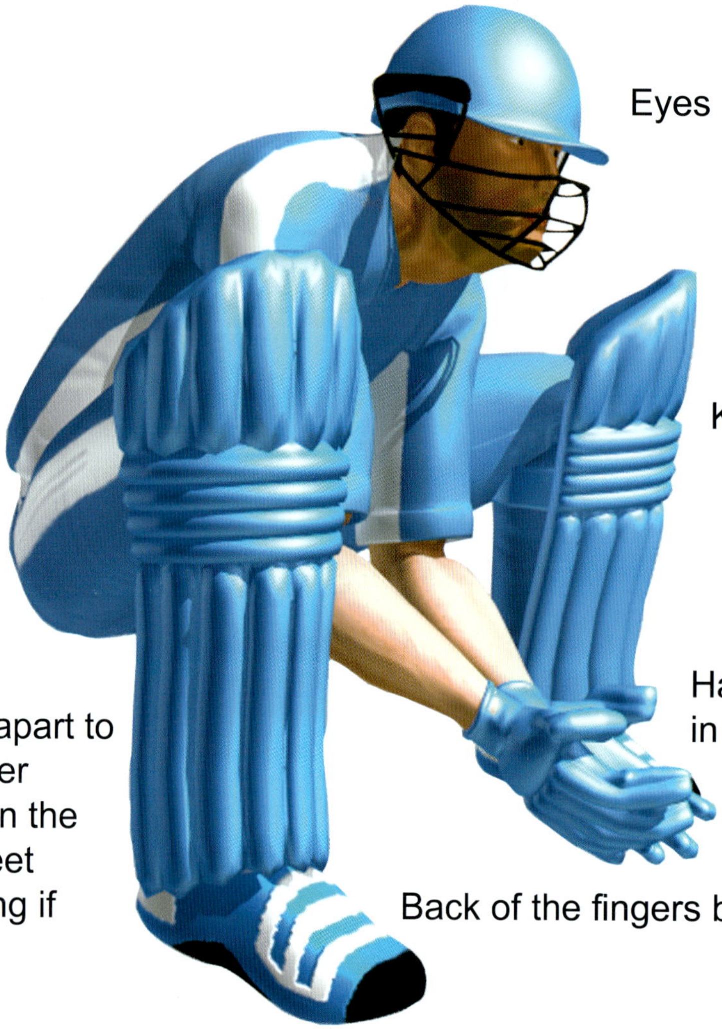

The keeper is ready to move in any direction to take the next ball.

STANDING BACK

A wicket-keeper needs to be able to see the entire flight of the ball. He/She must stand half or three-fourths of a pace behind the stumps just to the side of the off-stumps. In the case of a fast bowler, he/she must be even farther back. His distance behind the wickets should be such that he/she can take regular deliveries at a height between the waist and knees. It requires a lot of sense to judge. A keeper must get used to the bowler in practice before hand. In a game, he/she must get the right distance as early as possible. It is particularly important because slips take their position from the wicket-keeper.

TAKING THE BALL

A wicket-keeper should never try to move before the ball has pitched but only once. After it, he/she will have a good idea of the ball's path towards the wickets. Most balls should come through on the off-side but the keeper must be ready for a leg-side delivery. The idea behind it is to move a bit late but very quickly. Eyes must be kept on the ball, not on the batsman. Movement should be in line with the ball. Take on the ball smoothly keeping the arms almost straight but relaxed. As soon as the ball comes into the cupped gloves, the elbows must be bent to cushion its landing. Then the hands should slide with the ball travelling back with it. The body-weight must be placed on the foot nearest to the wicket.

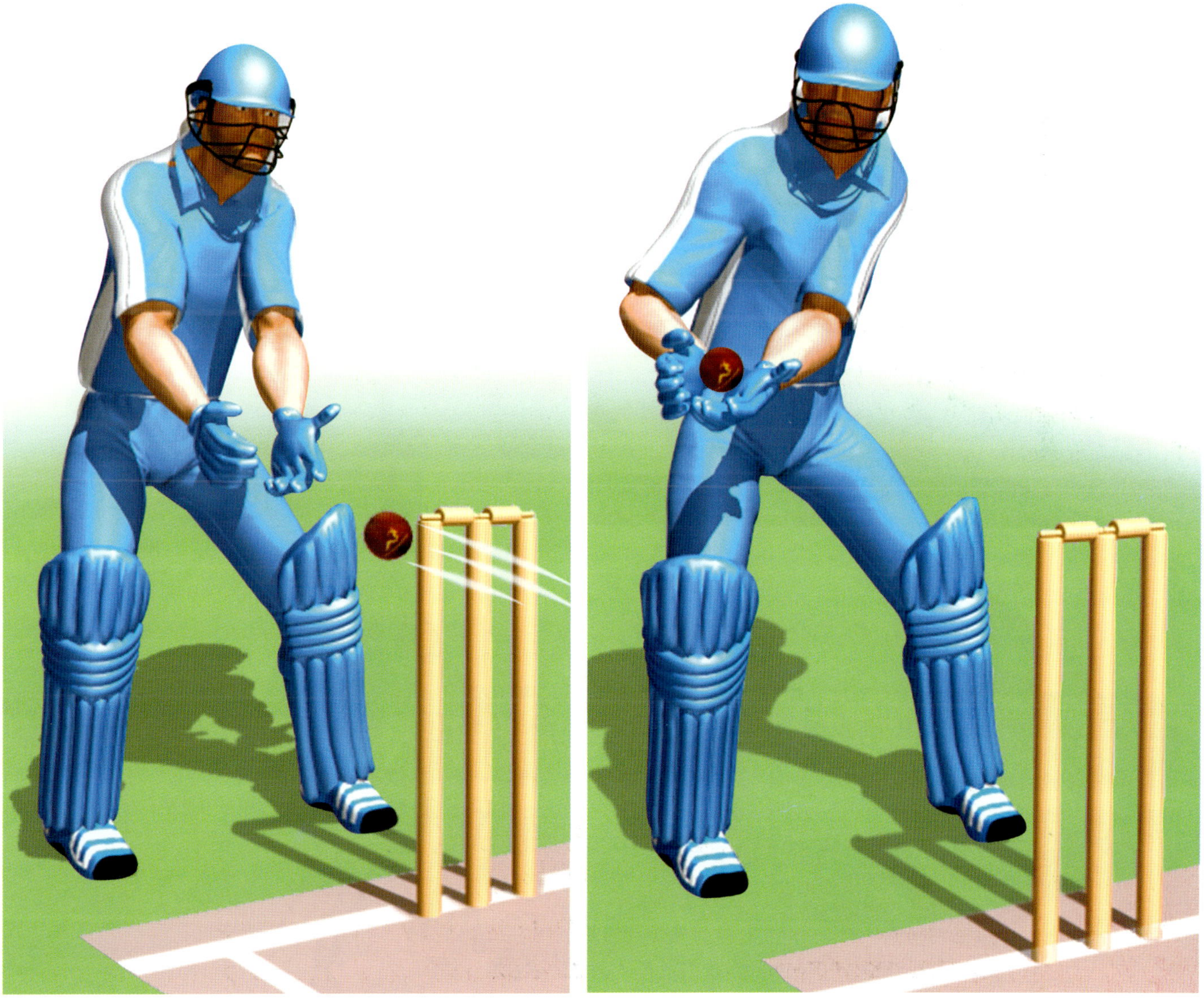

The fingers of a wicket-keeper should never point directly at the ball. Because there is every possibly of breaking the fingers and be out of the game.

POOR VIEW

Batsmen annoy wicket-keepers not only by reducing the chance of taking practice hitting the ball before it reaches the keeper but also by blocking the keeper's view just when the ball is coming to him. That is partly why the keeper needs to move only once to have a good idea of where the ball is heading for.

Even if the batsman is doing well and is hitting every delivery, the wicket-keeper should expect every ball to come through to him/her. As an innings progresses, the keeper should keep on stretching between the overs. It is sure to keep him or her supple and loose.

HIGH RISER

Sometimes a ball rises higher than it is expected. The wicket-keeper should use his/her body to turn to the side and keep his or her hands behind the ball while making a high take.

HIGH TAKE

The high or overhead take is needed when a bouncer or top edge of the bat causes the ball to rise above body height. In this case, the eyes should be kept squarely on the ball and the arms and fingers should point to a 12 o' clock position of the clock-arms. Many a wicket-keeper finds it desirable to catch the ball with his/her stronger hand pushing the other hand behind it for support.

SOME BASIC PRACTICE-MOVES

Whenever a few friends are at practice—batting or bowling, a wicket-keeper should put on his/her gloves and join in.

LEG-SIDE DRILL

Most deliveries come down the off-side but a new wicket-keeper may have a problem in the case of a leg-side delivery. Here is a handy practice for a keeper and one or more of the keeper's friends.

The thrower aims at missing the wicket.

The wicket-keeper should ask a friend to throw a ball such that it travels outside the leg-stump. Then he should work on moving across to take the ball in a clean way. He/She should then ask the friend to throw the ball such that it pitches further and further up the pitch towards the keeper. Once, the wicket-keepers feels comfortable while taking the balls pitching on the crease, he/she must add a batsman who does not hit the ball but just obstructs the keeper's view as it happens in a real match.

POSITION DRILL

A wicket-keeper can practise without wearing gloves and pads. He should ask a friend to stand about 10 metres away and throw a tennis ball or any other soft ball overarm such that it bounces once before reaching the wicket-keeper. The thrower should be asked to vary the throw as the keeper gets more confident. The thrower can come up with faster balls letting then travel leg-side or over the wicket.

DON'T FEEL UPSET

Every wicket-keeper not only misses catches but also lets ordinary deliveries go past him/her. Such a delivery gets to the boundary for four runs. Unlike other fielders who may be left to feel unpleasant for several overs, the wicket-keeper must not get upset about it at all. He/She has to concentrate on the next delivery learning a lesson and putting the error out of the mind.

FANCY STUFF

DIVES

It is very difficult to teach the diving technique through a book. The only way to achieve it is—PRACTICE. An old mattress or, if at school, a crash mat from the gym, is ideal for soft landing during dives.

Nice dive, Wayne ! The only trouble is that you don't keep your eyes on the ball.

STUMPING

Stumping chances are rare but the wicket-keeper must be alert to the possibility. He/She should get into the routine of collecting the ball and passing it close to the stumps in a single action. Stumping is only a slight extension of that movement.

FIELDING AND RUN-OUTS

As soon as a batsman has hit the ball, the wicket-keeper should get behind the wicket quite ready to receive the throw from the fielder. He must always try to stay within striking distance of the stumps. If the batsman is struggling to get back into his crease, the keeper should look to collect the ball and knock off the bails as quickly and smoothly as possible.

The wicket-keeper's action is a single smooth, continuous movement.

The wicket-keeper must watch each and every throw from a fielder. If it is not quite accurate, he/she should try to make ground to catch it smoothly. It is sure to boost the fielder's morale and help the keeper stay alert—ready for the next catch or even stumping chance.

Chapter Nine

Captaining A Side

It is not that a cricket match is always won by the side with best or more experienced players. The winning side is the team that plays with a deep team spirit ; that adapts itself to the conditions and forcefully reacts to the efforts of the opposing side. And all these factors can be handled only by the captain of a side better than any other player.

CAPTAINING A SIDE

Though it is great honour to be captain of a team, yet it involves great skill and understanding. It needs observation and judgement along with patience and strategy. In short, it is an art worth mastering. The captain of a junior side must not worry about declarations, follow-ons etc. But he/she has a lot to do—from winning the toss and deciding whether to bat or field first to choosing the order for his batsmen to play or placing them for fielding.

KNOWING THE PLAYERS

A good captain must have a good knowledge of all the rules of the game as well as the real knowledge of the strengths and weaknesses of his/her players. He/She must not feel bullied by most confident-looking and boasting players as they are always the best. He/She must stick to his decisions that are to be made taking the advice of the team-mates.

THINKING ABOUT THE TEAM

1. Who are the fastest fielders ? They can be out in the covers or at mid-wickets ?
2. Who are the best at close catching ? They must be in the slips or in close catching position.
3. Which players can score runs quickly ?
4. Which players are the best defensive batsmen ?
5. How long can the best strike-bowler bowl ?
6. Who are the most accurate bowlers—not essentially wicket-taking ones ?

A captain is only as good as his/her team. Even the world's best captain cannot win a match without decent bowlers and batsmen. Inversely, an efficient team handled badly, can let the match slip out of their hands.

CAPTAINCY AND FIELDING

Good captaincy is really important as far as fielding is concerned. It is the captain who decides which player is to bowl and when as well as for how long. He/She also decides where to place the fielders, i.e. setting of the field. A captain must stay calm and composed throughout the game encouraging his team-mates all the time.

PICKING AND SHUFFLING THE BOWLING

A captain is lucky enough to have two or three good bowlers. They should be allowed to bowl and hopefully watch the wickets fall. The real test for a captain is when the wickets do not fall, the best bowlers get tired and more high-quality bowlers are not there.

The captain should keep the bowling varying using all this bowlers with sagacity. There are no hard and fast rules for captaining a winning side. Had there been any, every captain would have followed them and cricket would have become a very dull game indeed. Still the common ploy is to use the attacking bowler at one end while the most accurate bowler at the other end to keep the batsman tied.

ASKING FOR ADVICE

Though it is the captain who has to take all decisions, yet it doesn't mean that he/she mustn't ask his team-mates for advice. As far as fielding is concerned, the wicket-keeper is the best person to be consulted. The reason is that he/she is the one most line in with the bowler and the batsman on the crease. He knows how fast the ball is coming to him and knows best if the bowler is getting tired and his/her deliveries are slowing. Besides, the wicket-keeper has the best knowledge of how the pitch is working.

SETTING THE FIELD

For want of space, no comprehensive guidance can be given in this book for all fielding settings. Even then three basic placings can be given.

1. Placing should be different for each bowler according to his type and merit.
2. No hard and fast rules are there for placings.
3. The captain should use his judgement and direction as far as fielding is concerned.

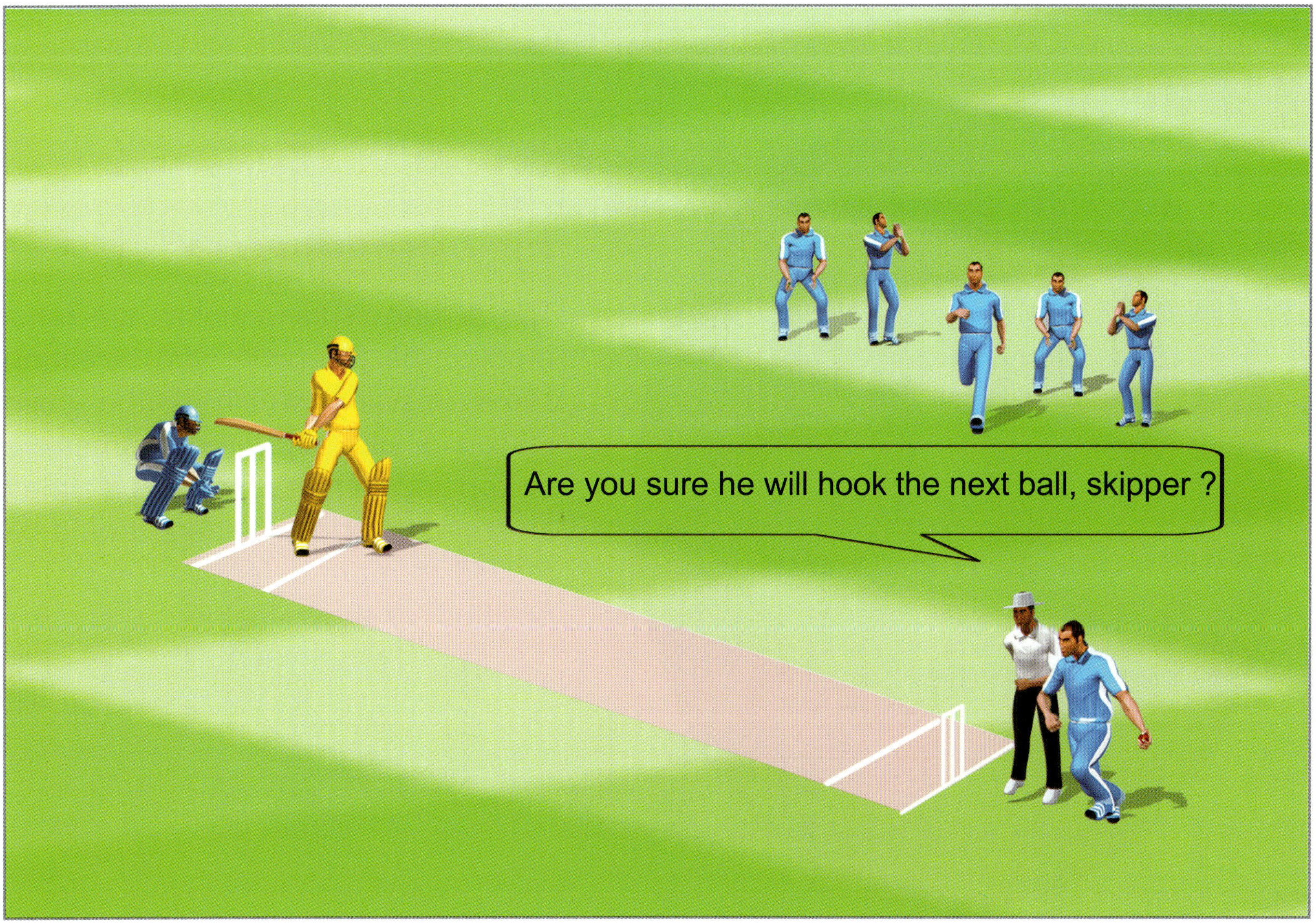

FIELDING POSITIONS

FOR A FAST BOWLER

Shown below is a suggested basic field-setting for a fast bowler pitching the ball on or around the off-stumps. And all these field-settings are for a right-handed batsman. The short-square-leg position is for catches that may come off bat and pad.

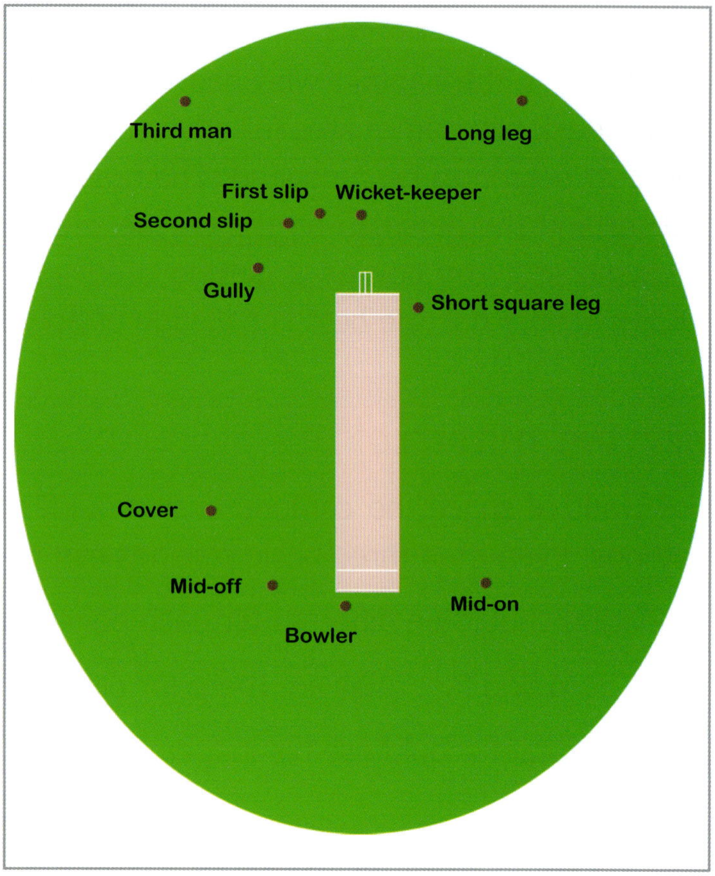

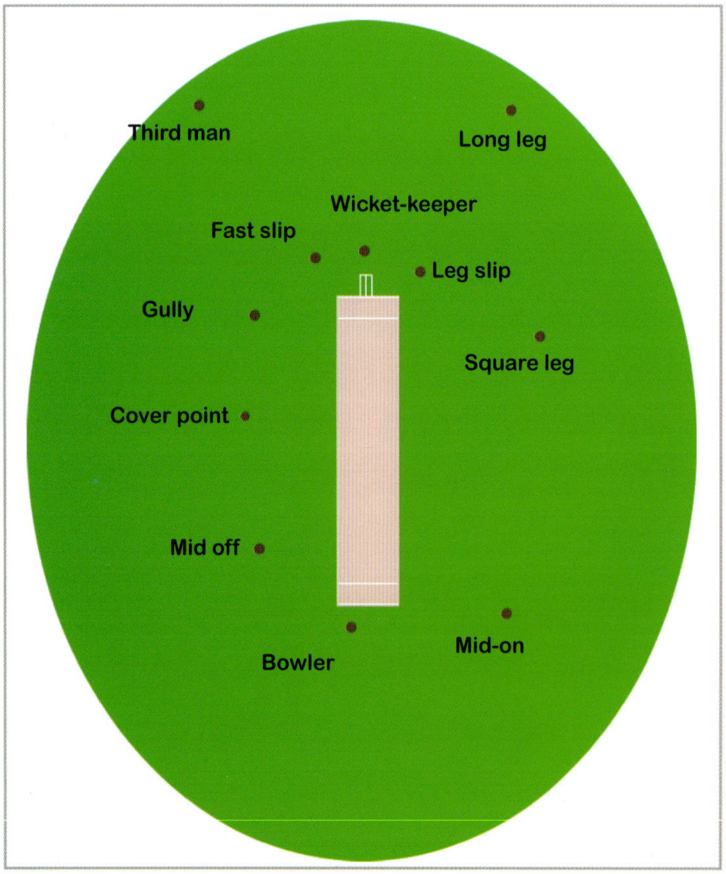

FOR A MEDIUM-PACER

The settings shown below are for a medium-paced bowler who is creating some in-swing which is the main reason for a leg slip. If the batsmen are on top and restricting of runs is aimed at, several of close fielders should be moved to more defensive run-saving positions as shown below.

FOR AN OFF-SPIN BOWLER

An off-spinner is always up to look for mishits and mistimed strokes that result in catches by fielders. In this case, the field is to be fairly defensive. But if the ball is turning sharply and the batsman looks uncomfortable against the spin, the captain must go in for more attack. Two sensibly attacking suggestions are—

1. To move the extra-cover fielder closer to the wicket.
2. To move the fine-leg fielder closer to the wicket.

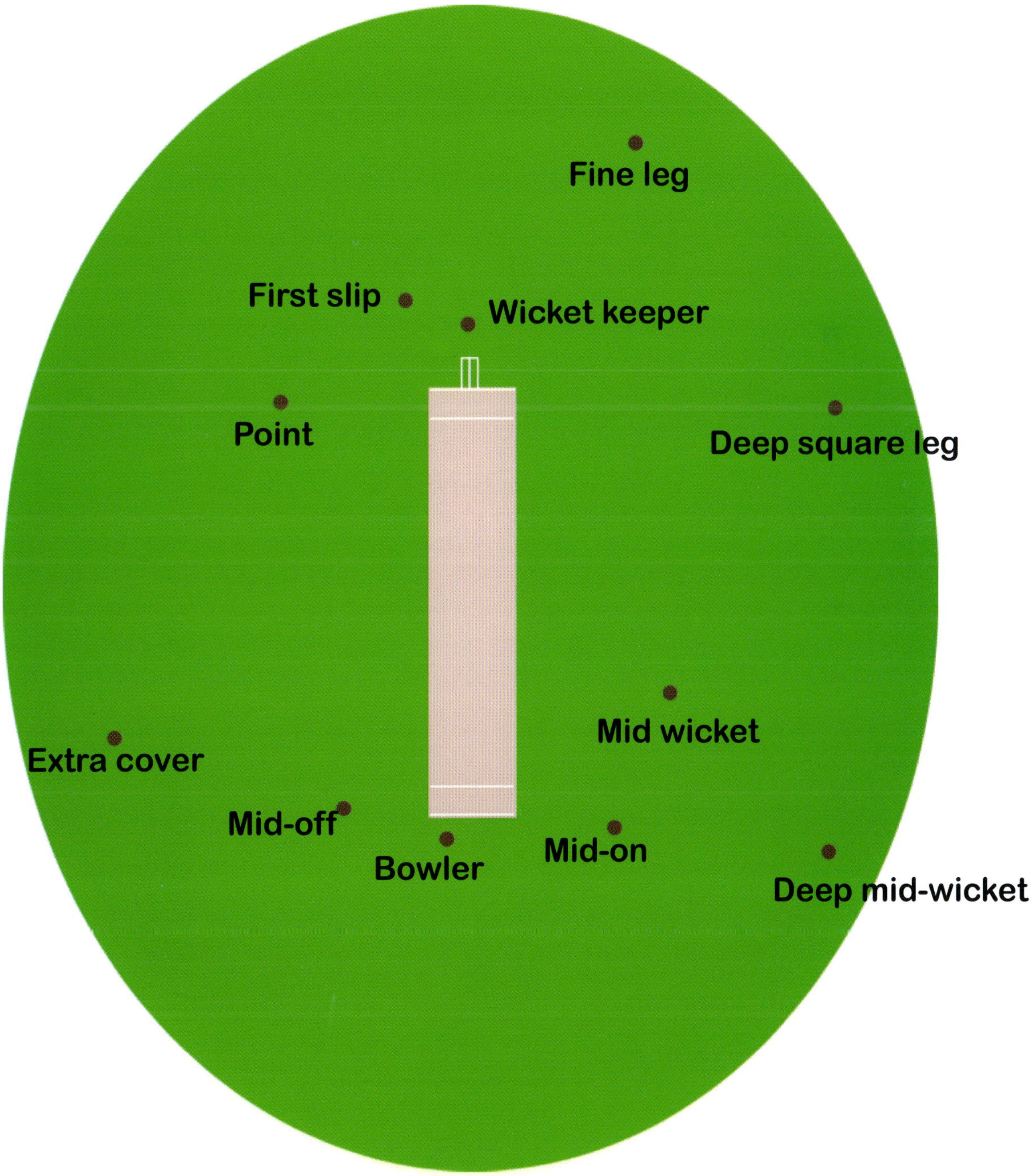

CRICKET FIELDING POSITIONS

Familiarise yourself with cricket fielding positions from the diagram on this page.

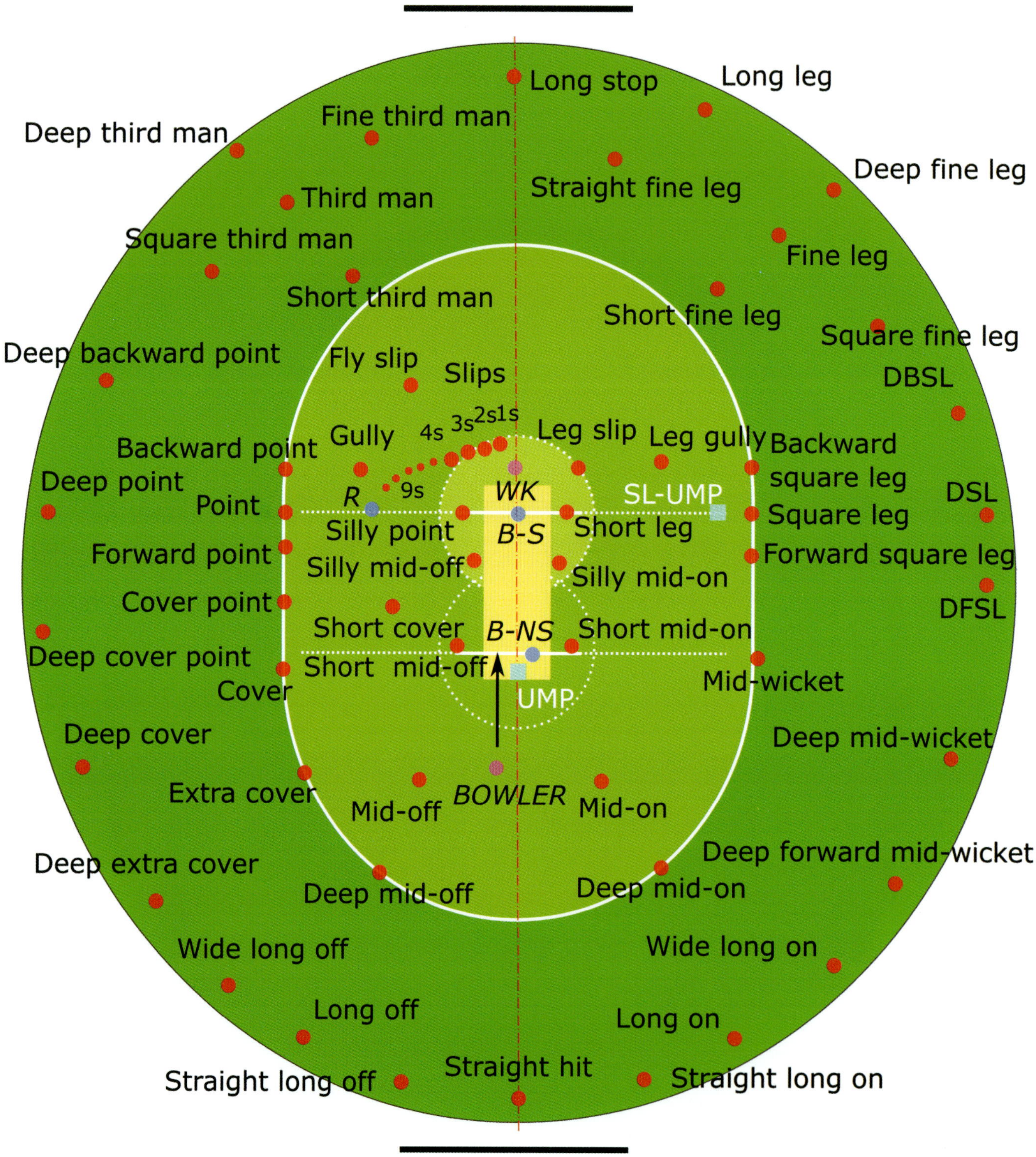

LEARNING FROM OTHERS

A captain who is desirous of picking up tips about field-setting, captaincy and other important jobs of a captain should learn from the best captains and players by listening to what they have said in their books, on T.V., or radio. Captains like Clive Lloyed, Allan Border and Mike Brearley knew their jobs thoroughly.

Watching live test matches or first class cricket is not only great fun but a source to learn as well. A top-class fast bowler's speed and power and timing of an experienced batsman are really amazing for any viewer.

If a live watch is beyond reach, TV or radio coverage can serve as a good substitute. The radio commentaries by famous commentators are really beneficial. As for T.V., its wonderful camera work and action replays and views from the cameras inside the stumps called stump-cams serve as good teachers.

Chapter Ten

Competition Cricket

FIRST-CLASS CRICKET

First-class cricket is the serious stuff, often played by professionals. No match is more serious and important than a test match. Playing in a test match makes a cricketer reach the pinnacle of his game career. Each match is played over five days and there is often a three-, five- or six-match series to determine the ultimate winner.

THE ASHES

The most famous of all the test-match competitions, the Ashes is a bitter battle between two countries—England and Australia. It started when Australia beat England in a test-match series for the first time in 1882. A newspaper joked that English cricket had died and would be cremated. The Ashes (of a burnt bail) are permanently stationed at the Lords. But the title, remains shifting between England and Australia depending on who is the winner of the latest series.

DOMESTIC CHAMPIONSHIPS

All cricket-playing nations have their own internal leagues in the form of counties, states or regional sides. They play domestic cricket for a trophy. In Britain, it is the County Championship while in Australia it is the famous Shieffield Shield. In India it is the Ranji Trophy. These games are first class cricket over three or four days with two innings either side in case time and weather permit.

A FIRST-CLASS DAY

Play is split into three sessions—each being two hours long. There is a break for lunch, another for tea and still another 10-minute break for changeover between the innings. A minimum number of overs are to be bowled in a full day and a complex set of rules are there to be followed in case a full day's play isn't possible or if any side bowls slowly.

FIRST-CLASS CRICKET TACTICS

If all innings have not been completed by the end of the final day, i.e. when the stumps are to be drawn, the game ends in a draw. The time-limit can lead to some interesting possibilities for the captains of the two sides.

A FOLLOW-ON

If the side batting second achieves a much smaller score than that of the first side, the second team may have to play the second innings immediately. It is called a follow-on. Scoring considerable runs to pass the follow-on target is vital for the struggling side. This target is usually 150 or 200 runs diminished from the first team's total. Also, it causes the second team to bat again which eats up time but may help the struggling team avoid a defeat.

DECLARATIONS

If a side is able to build up a big total, its captain may declare the innings to be closed before all of his batsman have been out. The aim behind it is to allow enough time to win the match. Many captains time their declarations such that only a difficult half hour or so is left for the batsmen of the opposing team to play before lunch, tea or the end of that day's play.

CONTRIVED FINISH

It sometimes happens when time is short and both the sides are really eager for a win. What happens in such a case is that one side forgoes an innings or bowls gently to allow the other side to build up a reasonable total but with an unspoken agreement to declare the game. It sets up a potential win for either side.

Some old fogeys condemn this arrangement saying that it is "just not cricket," though it allows a competitive end to a game and great fun and excitement for the spectators.

ONE-DAY CRICKET

A one-day game gives each side one innings in which to score more runs than the other side does. The overs that either side has to bat can vary in number—20 in some school games or charity matches, 40 in some Club League Games and 50, 55 or 60 into first class competitions.

CHANGES AND CHANGES

Many changes have been introduced in one-day cricket. These changes aim at drawing bigger crowds and at popularising cricket as a game. Some of the changes include—

(a) playing at night under artificial light

(b) using a white-ball

(c) use of different coloured kits for various teams That is why it is often referred to pyjama games.

THE WORLD CUP

It is the ultimate in one-day cricket. All cricket-playing countries participate in this exciting competition that is played once every four years. 50-over games for every side are played at Group Stages followed by knock-out rounds and further leading to the final competition.

TEAM SELECTION

All-rounders who can bat and bowl efficiently manage to be picked up for one-day games. Batsmen who are big hitters are prompted upwards in the batting order in order to build up scores as quickly as possible. The players who possess the nerve to bat and bowl well during the last few overs of a side's innings are specially prized. Some nations have special one-day captains and squads—different from their test-match captains and squads.

ONE-DAY SKILLS

Here are a few skills that are useful to successful one-day players and teams.

FIELDING AND BOWLING

For bowlers, though it is still important to take wickets, yet keeping the run-rate down is even more important. It needs accurate bowlers to keep the quality batsmen pinned down by dint of intelligent bowling. Umpires are far stricter to wide balls in one-day games than in the first class test matches.

One-day games have really sharpened fielding skills. The best fielders are always on the look-out for catches and run-outs. Every single run matters in a one-day game as it can turn the game to any of the two sides.

ONE-DAY BATTING

It is vital to keep the score moving along and for it, fast running between the wickets is the key-note. It has often been seen that the lower-order batsman try all types of strange shots to score runs quickly. It happens in the later overs of the game. It makes many coaches shut their eyes and shudder.

THE 15-OVER CIRCLE

The 28m (30 yard) circle marked around the wicket is the biggest difference between the rules for first class games and one-day games. In a one-day game, for the first 15 overs, not more than two fielders can be placed outside the 28m circle. It surely promotes aggressive batting early on.

PINCH HITTING

A pinch hitter is an aggressive opening batsman who tries his/her best to accumulate runs fast by hitting safely over the heads of the fielders standing inside the 28m circle. Sanath Jayasurya has the credit of revolutionising the pinch-hitting. A fine regular batsman, with 340 as his highest score, he ruined England's chances in the World Cup of 1995/96 hammering 82 runs in 44 balls. He is also credited with scoring the fastest 50 in one-day internationals. He did it just in 17 balls playing against Pakistan.

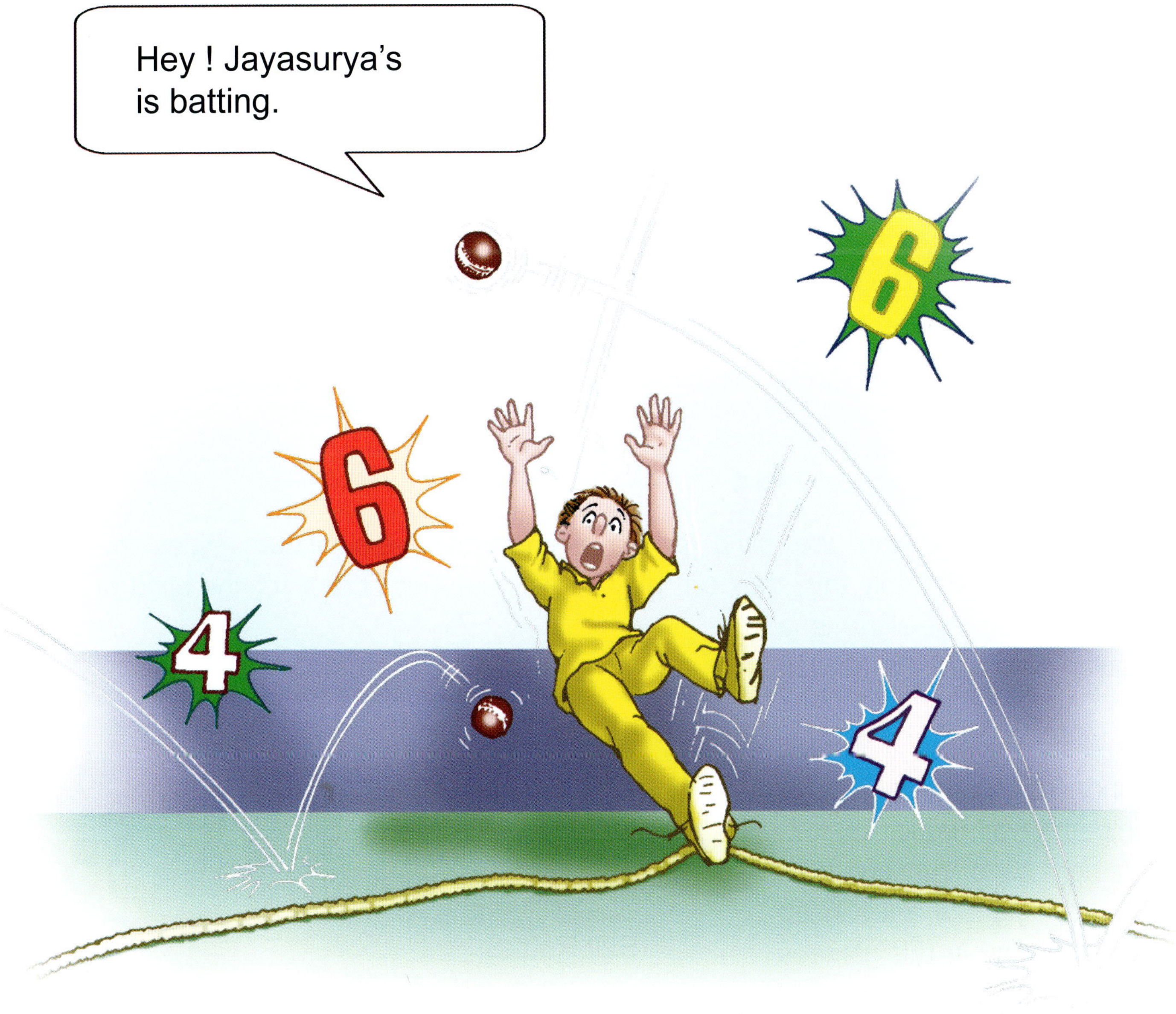

INDOOR CRICKET

Indoor cricket is an excitingly fast-moving game played indoors during winter. But in Britain, it is played during summer too. It is played on a 30m by 10m astroturf pitch surrounded by nets. Each team has eight players and each batsman bats for 4 overs only and loses five runs if he is out. Each bowler bowls only two overs. Batsmen can score runs in the normal way—hitting the ball and running just half the length of a full-size pitch. Apart from it, they can score boundaries placing the ball into special areas. But they can be caught out off the net surrounding the pitch.

KWIK CRICKET

This cricket is a selection of different games—all played with a special cricket set designed for younger players. It is made of hard-wearing materials and is light as well as safe enough to allow cricket to be played without pads and other protectors as also indoors or outdoors.

CRICKET FOR SPECIAL NEEDS

The cricket fans who are blind or have impaired eye-sight are aided by radio commentaries. Not only this, they can play cricket too. This cricket for the blind or those with impaired eye-sight is a popular sport. It is played with helpers and a large ball that produces a rattling sound. This game is just as competitive as regular cricket. Batsmen have runners with good eye-sight if they need them. Bowling in this game is underarm bowling.

IPL (Indian Premier League)

Launched as well as promoted by the Board of Control for Cricket in India (BCCI), Indian Premier League (IPL) made its debut in April 2008. Based on the English Premier League (football) and the National Basketball League (NBA) of the United States, IPL is a professional Twenty20 cricket league where different franchise teams participate for the title. It has been backed by the ICC and has a total of eight teams, with each of them being made up of a minimum of 16 players. It is the most-watched Twenty20 cricket league in the worlds and also known for its commercial success. It is currently sponsored by Pepsi and thus officially known as the Pepsi Indian Premier League.

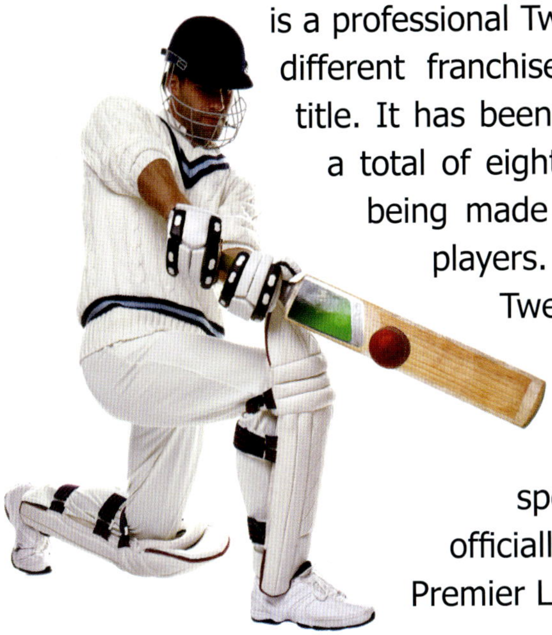

Chapter Eleven

Knocking in a cricket bat

READY POSITION FORWARD DEFENCE THE COVER DRIVE THE ON DRIVE

THE OFF SPIN

BACK-FOOT-DEFENCE THE SWEEP THE STRAIGHT

Chapter Twelve

More About Cricket

THE BAT

A cricket bat is a specialized equipment used by batsmen. It is usually made of white willow and has a rubber handle. The flat side is used to hit the ball.

Choosing the correct size bat is vital for proper technical development of young cricketers. It is important that the bat is not too long and more importantly, not too heavy to hinder correct stroke play and good technique. Junior Bats are sealed down in size and weight to meet this important requirement.

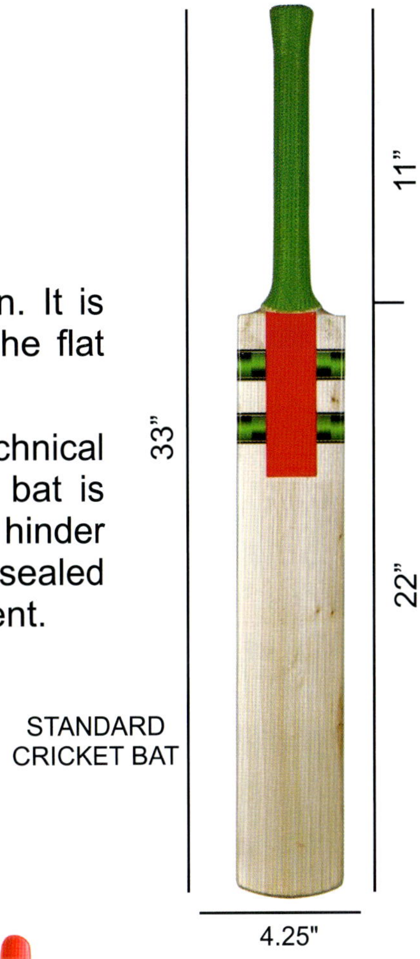

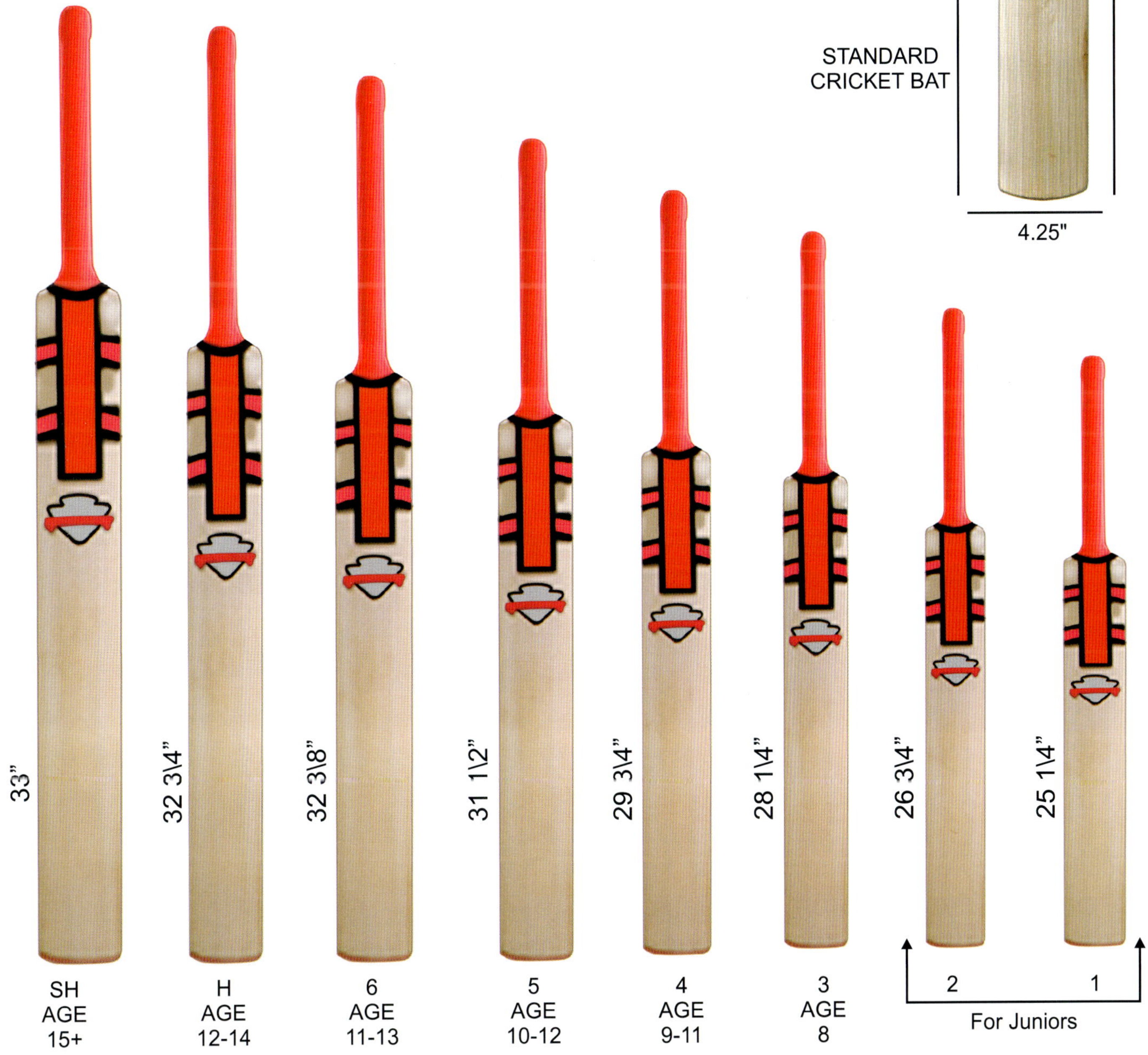

TIPS TO CHOOSE A CRICKET BAT

There are different models of bat available in the market. When it comes to buying a new cricket bat there are a number of factors that one should take into consideration before making a final decision, such as -The brand, -The size, -The model, -The weight.

You should choose carefully the model of cricket bat that most suitably fits your style of play. There are bats designed keeping in mind specific style of batting adopted by cricket players.

Next-importance is choosing the correct size of your bat. As a bat that is too large or too small will hinder your playing ability.

The weight of a cricket bat is most important. One should start off playing with a light weight bat and then switch over to heavier bat as one gains proficiency. Generally, an adult should choose a weight around 2'8-2'10 oz, is a short handle (SH).

100 PLUS

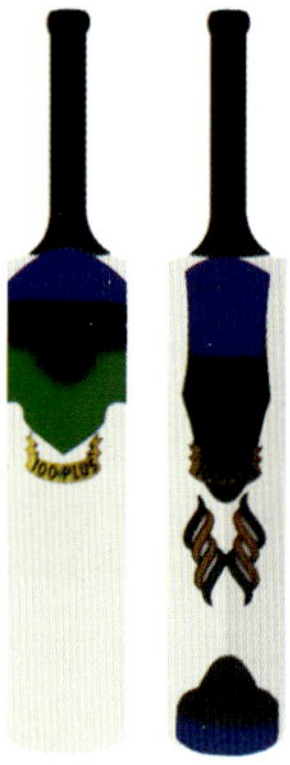

TOP GRADE
WEIGHT 1200-1250gms.
LENGTH 85 cms
WIDTH 11 cms
BLADE 5.5 cms Approx.
GRAINS 12-16
FLEXIBLE CANE HANDLE
WITH TOE GUARD
& COVER

RAJA

TOP GRADE
WEIGHT 1200-1250gms.
LENGTH 85 cms
WIDTH 11 cms
BLADE 5.5 cms Approx.
GRAINS 12-16
FLEXIBLE CANE HANDLE
WITH TOE GUARD
& COVER

JUMBO

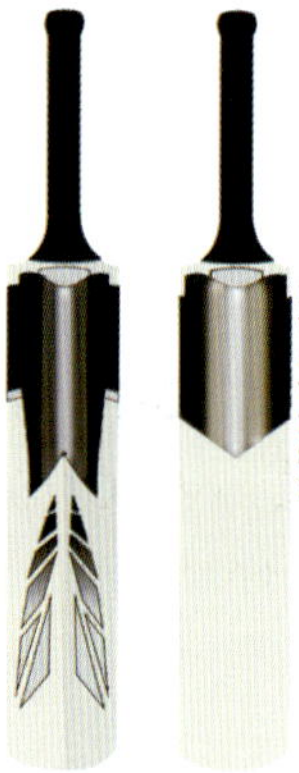

MEDIUM GRADE
WEIGHT 1250-1300 gms
LENGTH 85 cms
WIDTH 11 cms
BLADE 4.5-5 cms
SEMI GRAINED
FLEXIBLE CANE HANDLE

WILLOW KING

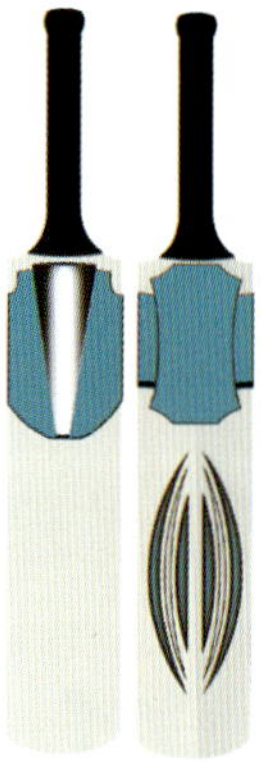

PRACTISE QUALITY
WEIGHT 1250-1350 gms
LENGTH 85 cms
WIDTH 11 cms
BLADE 4-5 cms
CANE HANDLE

X-FACTOR

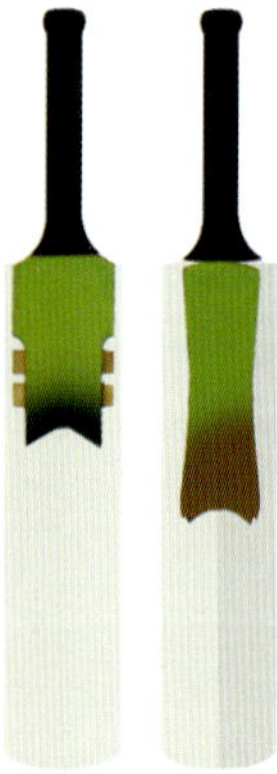

KASHMIR WILLOW
POPULAR HANDLE
WEIGHT 1250-1350gms
LENGTH 85 cms
WIDTH 11 cms

BLASTER

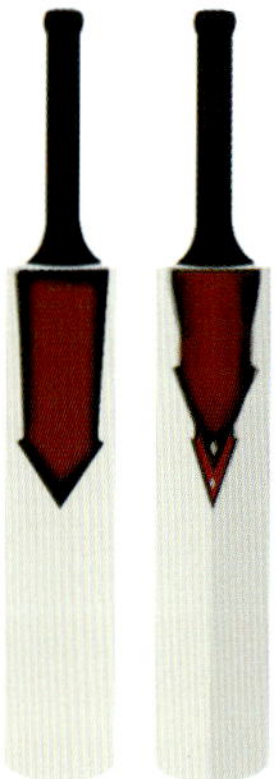

TENNIS BAT
WITH SCOOP
POPULAR HANDLE
LENGTH 85 cms
WIDTH 11-13 cms

STATUS

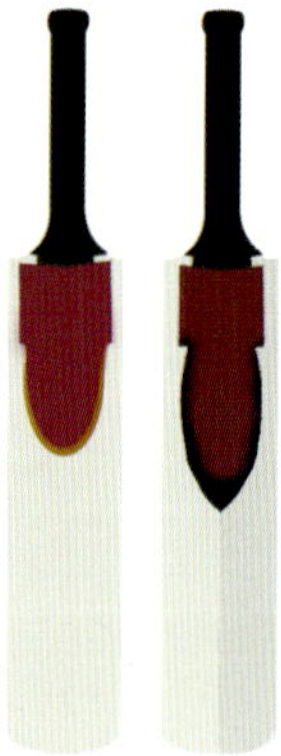

POPULAR WILLOW
POPULAR HANDLE

HARD HITER

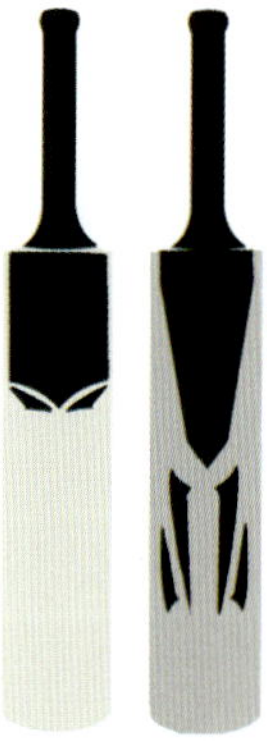

DUCO PAINTED
POPULAR WOOD
SILVER/BLACK BACK
ATTRACTIVE DESIGN

CRICKET BAT KNOCKING HAMMER

Knocking the bat with a cricket bat knocking hammer help prevent damage from the impact of a cricket ball. Knocking in should be done in a thorough manner patiently. The fibers of the willow blade get compressed and knitted together by this process.

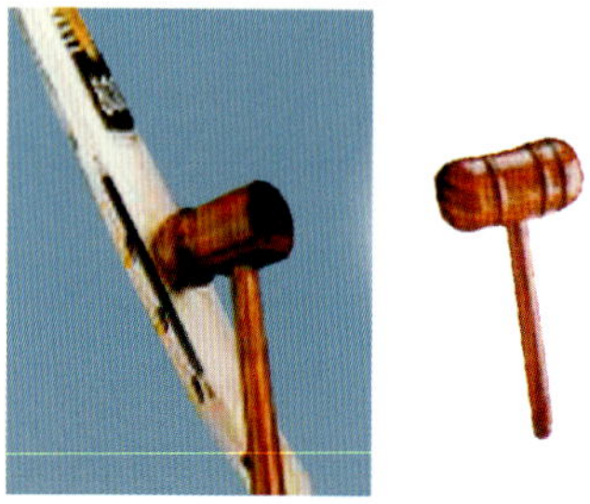

CRICKET BAT KNOCKING HAMMER

The Mongoose bat or MMi3 is a cricket bat specifically designed for Twenty-20 cricket.

The dimensions of a standard cricket bat and mongoose bat are:

Standard Cricket Bat	Mongoose Cricket Bat
Total Length – 33-33.5 inches	Total Length – 31 inches
Handel Length – 11inches	Handel Length – 15.8 inches
Batting part – 22 inches	Batting part – 14.5 inches
Width – 4.25 inches	Width – 4.5 inches
Thickness – 1 Inch	Thickness – 1 Inch

MONGOOSE CRICKET BAT

THE BALL

The cricket ball is very hard, covered in red leather and stitched. It weighs between 5.5 oz. (155-9gms) to 5.75 oz. (163 gm) and measures between 8.11 inches (22.4cm.) to 9 inches (22.9cm) in circumference.

THE WICKETS

The wicket includes three stumps and two bails upon the top, at either end of the pitch. The three stumps that are 28 inches (71.1cm) tall, positioned so they are 9 inches (23cm) wide topped with two bails each measuring 4-6 inches (11.1cm) in length. The wickets are hammered 3.1 inches (7.5cm) into the ground.

Stump cam is a tiny camera in both middle stumps positioned about half way up. This helps to determine whether the ball has struck the batsman, bat or pad. The technology helps the on-field umpire's decision making accuracy.

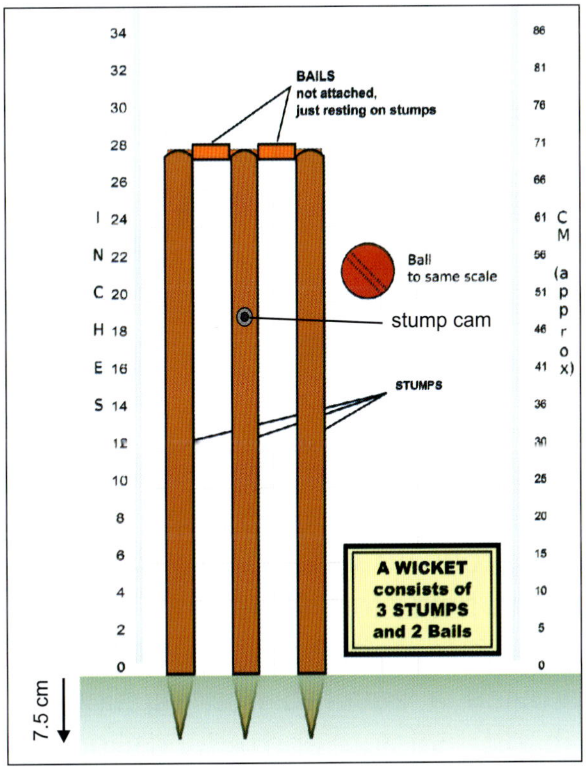

IMPORTANCE OF HELMET

In the game of cricket batsmen often wear a helmet to protect themselves from injury by the cricket ball. Without proper protection injuries can be severe. Raman Lamba died while fielding at silly point without a helmet. He got hit on the head. Hence, helmet with cage and chin guard has an utmost importance for batsmen, fielders and a wicketkeeper.

IMPORTANCE OF PADS

Pads are protective equipment used by batsmen and a wicket-keeper in the sports of cricket. Pads protect the legs from impact by a hard ball.

Batting pads are large, protecting shins, knees and a lower of knees with a slot for the foot. Wicketkeeper's pads are smaller than batting pads, with significant knee flaps.

IMPORTANCE OF GLOVES

When you are playing cricket at speed, you are prone to get hit on wrist and hands. Same holds true for a wicket-keeper. Thus the gloves are highly necessary. Gloves provide a secured non slipping grip and absorb moisture and reduce slippage.

CRICKET SHOES

Cricket shoes should be light weight, flexible and highly cushioned. Such shoes give a great leap forward in players comfort and protection. Rounded contours of the shoe soles protect the player and improve their performance.

PHYSIOLOGY AND ENERGY SYSTEM IN CRICKET

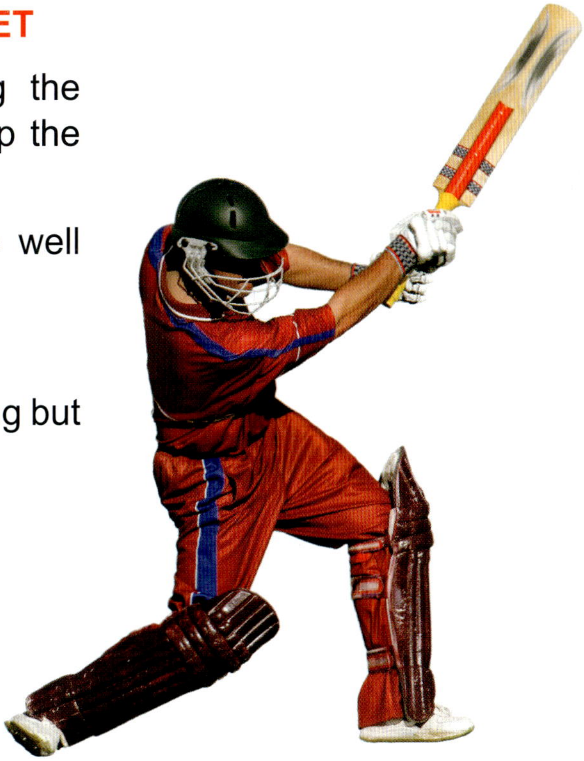

One needs to be fit to play cricket. Achieving the appropriate level of fitness each player must keep the following points in consideration:

He must not over train in practice and must be well relaxed before the game.

He should exercise mildly on off days.

He may swim, play tennis or golf in the early morning but should stay out of the midday sun.

To develop one's stamina-

He should run, skip or cycle for 10 to 20 minute.

He should do push-ups, sit ups and swing the bat.

Many new ideas have developed in the recent years like cardiovascular, aerobic or endurance fitness. The aim of these new ideas is to achieve progressive adaptation to the demands of the game and to minimum the risk of injury and burn out.

These different aspects of fitness techniques will vastly improve crickets skill.

BALANCED DIET

Cricket is played over one or more days, hence meal is part of the schedule of the game. Maintaining a healthy diet including plenty of fruit and vegetables with adequate amount of water ensure players to be energetic and maintain correct hydration level. The following food pyramid shows ideal proportion of food that a player should take daily.

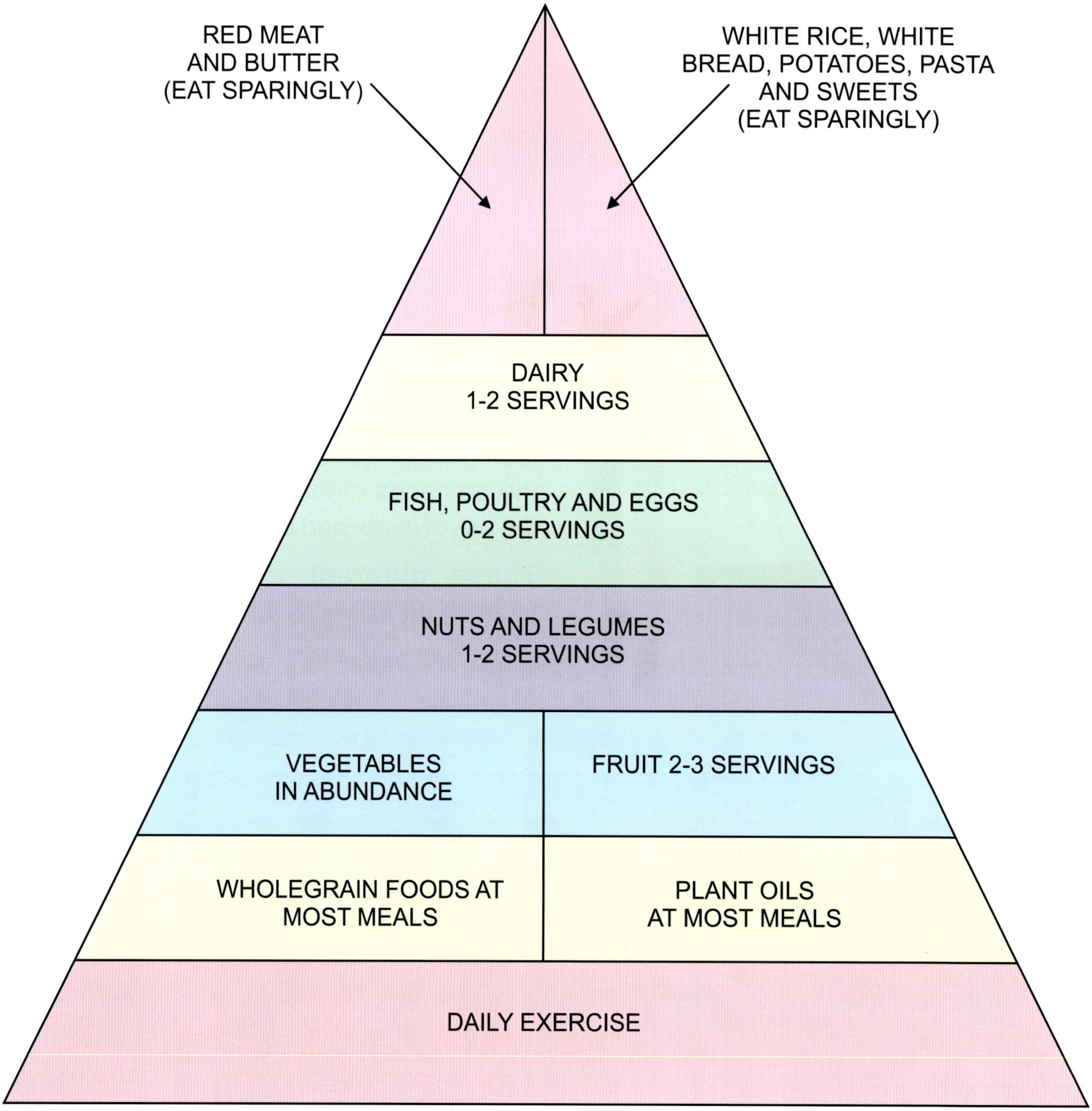

CRICKET ACCESSORIES

BATTING LEGGUARDS

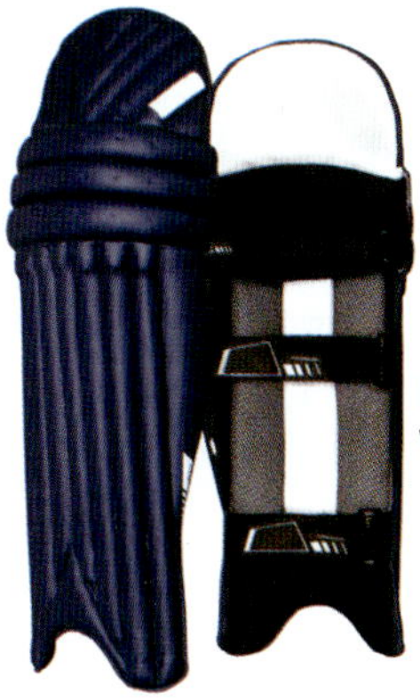

PU. FOAM PACKED
VELCRO BELTS

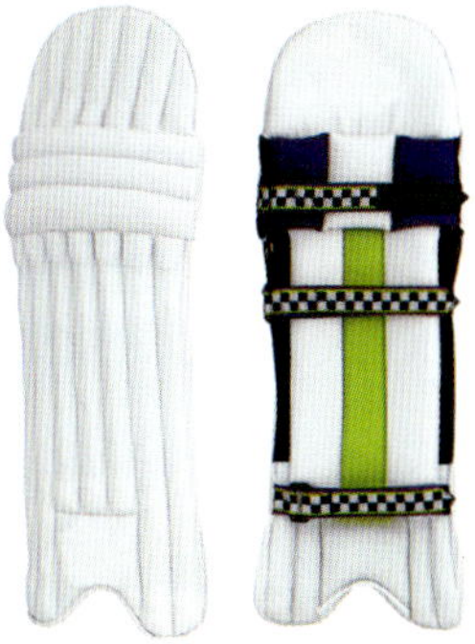

TETRON CLOT
COLOURS AVAIL

WICKET KEEPING PADS

TEST

CLASSIC

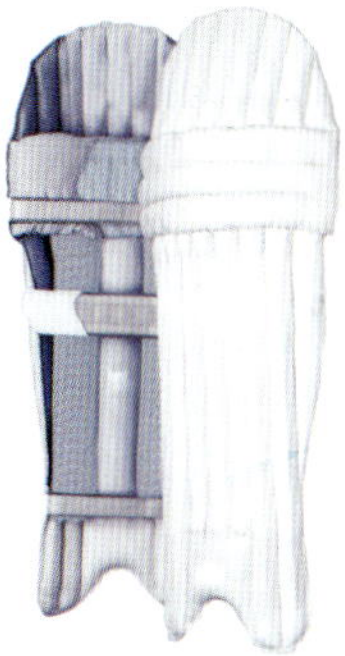

BATTING GLOVES

CLASSIC

PU. FOAM
LEATHER PALM

TEST

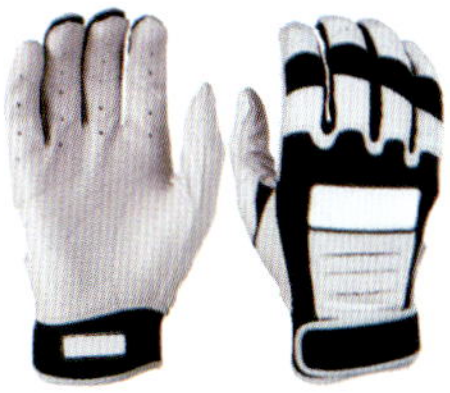

LIGHT WEIGHT FOAM

MATCH

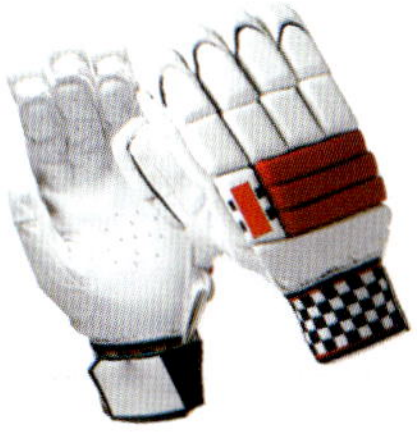

GOOD QUALITY FOAM

BATTING ACCESSORIES

THIGH GUARD

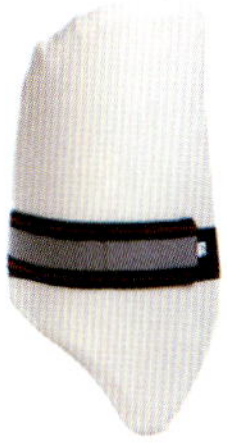

ARM GUARD

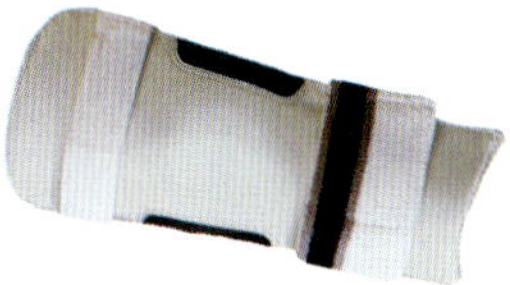

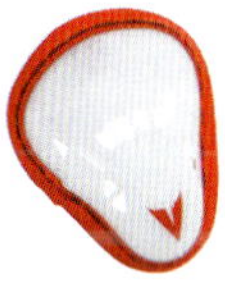

ABDOMINAL GURAD

WICKET KEEPING GLOVES

PERFECT

LEATHER
CONSTRUCTION

GUARD

SAMBER
LEATHER

CLUB

FOAM BACK
PRACTISE QUALITY

GRIP CONE WITH BRASS RING

CRICKET BAT GRIPS

OCTOPUS

COMBY

NUTTY

SPIRAL

BEND CHEVRON

MULTI

Chapter Thirteen

Record Holders

The history of cricket started hundreds of years ago during the 16th century. The game originated in southern England but today is popular in Australasia, England, the Indian subcontinent, the West Indies and Southern Africa. Since its early days cricket has produced many legendary players. Take a look at these best cricketers of all time.

Sir Don Bradman (Australia)
Sir Don Bradman is considered the greatest batsmen of all time as he averaged approximately 100 in test cricket.

Sachin Tendulkar (India)
This batting Guru has scored a hundred 100s' in his career, a record which seems to be unbreakable. He has the highest number of runs in both ODI and Test formats, with over 34, 000 runs under his belt. He is one of two players who are able to score a double century in an ODI match.

Gary Sobers (West Indies)
Gary Sober is one of the best all-rounders the world has ever witnessed. His temperament, class and test match batting average is above many legendary cricketers.

Vivians Richard (West Indies)
Richard is well renowned for his destructive and explosive batting skills. He averages 47+ in ODI with a SR of more than 90.

Kapil Dev (India)
Under the Captaincy of Kepil-Dev India won their first World Cup title in the year 1983. He was a gifted batsman along with phenomenal bowling skills. In short, Kapil was a genuine all-rounder.

Imran Khan (Pakistan)
Imran Khan led Pakistan towards 1992 world cup glory with his outstanding leadership and cricketing skills. He is considered one of the top notch bowling all-rounders.

Ian Botham (England)
Ian was the best all-rounder of the 1970's, and probably one of the best all-rounders England ever has produced.

Jacques Kallis (South Africa)
If we talk about the best all rounders, no one can beat the elegance and class of Jacque Kallis. He has scored over 24,000 runs with 500+ wickets in his career. His class is matchless.

Muttiah Muralitharan (Srilanka)
Muthiah the "king of swing" is undoubtedly one of the greatest off-spinners of all time. He took exactly 800 wickets in his test career, a record which seems to be unbreakable after the introduction of T20 edition.

Shane Warne (Australia)
Shane Warne is the greatest leg spinner of all time, and dodged the batsmen for 708 times in Test Cricket. His cricketing career is considered to be the benchmark for all the leg spinners.

Wasim Akram (Pakistan)
People remember Wasim Akram as the "King of Swing". A very destructive Pakistani bowler, who's bowling created serious problems for batsmen, he also scored 257 runs in an inning of Test match.

Brian Lara (West Indies)
Brian Lara is one of the paramount ODI and test batsmen of all times. Lara scored the highest 400 runs in an inning of test cricket and has dominated the best bowlers in the world.

Ricky Ponting (Australia)
Australia has won two consecutive world cups under his captaincy. He is one of the most stylish and classy batsmen and has dominated over all the best bowlers. Punter has scored 27,000+ runs and 71 centuries in his prolific career.

Sanath Jaysuriya (Sri Lanka)
Sanath is one of the greatest attacking openers of world cricket. He is considered one of the finest all-rounders of all time, due to his aggressive batting and spin bowling. He has played over 400 matches in ODI.

Glenn Donald McGrath (Australia)
McGrath is considered the top bowler of Australian and world cricket. He bowls with a mediums fast pace and holds the record of most wickets in World Cup.

Shaun Pollock (South Africa)
South Africa has produced two of the greatest all-rounders of all time. One is Pollock and the other is Jacque Kallis. Pollock was more of a bowling all-rounder, whose magical deliveries troubled all the great players. He took 421 wickets in test matches with an amazing average of 23.11.

Rahul Dravid (India)
Rahul Dravid has the best defensive technique in the world of cricket. He is also known as 'The Wall'. Dravid has scored 13,000+ runs in test cricket with an astonishing average of 52.31. He has passed a score of 50 runs 194 times in his career.

Steve Waugh (Australia)
Steve Waugh is one of the greatest captains and all-rounders of Australian cricket. He has represented Australia for 20 years and he has scored 10,000+ runs in Test cricket with a remarkable average of 51.06 (32 hundreds & 50 fifties).

Chris Gayle (West Indies)
When it comes to power, no player on this planet can hit the ball as hard as Gayle. He is a sensation whose batting is filled with extraordinary aggression.

Adam Gilchrist (Australia)
If anyone thinks of the best batting wicket-keeper, certainly the name of Adam Gilchrist comes to mind. He was an aggressive left hand batsman, who destroyed the front line bowling attack of all the best teams.

Dennis Lillee (Australia)
Dennis Lillee is renowned as one of the most lethal bowlers of all time.

Javed Miadad (Pakistan)
Miadad is one of the toughest cricketers of all time and his attitude has made him a standout in the sport.

Sir Richard John Hadlee (New Zealand)
Richard Hadlee is regarded as one of the greatest fast bowlers and all-rounders in cricketing history. A bowling all-rounder, in an 86-Test career he took 431 wickets (at the time the world record), and was the first bowler to pass 400 wickets, with an average of 22.29, and made 3124 Test runs at 27.16, including two centuries and 15 fifties.

Mahendra Singh Dhoni (India)
Mahendra Singh Dhoni has emerged as one of India's most successful captain this cricket crazy country has seen. The captain cool has led the team to many first under his captaincy. Dhoni led Team India to No. 1 in the ICC Test Rankings for the first time in December 2009 and also closed the gap with Australia in one-dayers after winning the coveted 2011 Cricket World Cup.

Andrew Flintoff (England)
Andrew Flintoff widely Known as 'Freddie' He is best known for his heroics in the 2005 Ashes series that saw England win the Ashes for the first time since the 1986/87 season, A fast bowler capable of bowling in excess of 140 Kilometers per hour, Flintoff took 226 wickets at an average of 32.78.

Graeme Smith (South Africa)
A left-handed batsman, Graeme Smith is a remarkable story of courage, fortitude, conviction and tremendous leadership. He scored back-to-back double centuries on the 2003 tour of England, including a national record.

Test Records: Most Runs

Player's Name	Matches	Runs	100s	50s
Sachin Tendulkar	200	15921	51	68
Ricky Ponting	168	13378	41	62
Jacques Kalls	166	13289	45	58
Rahul Dravid	164	13288	36	63
Brian Lara	131	11953	34	48
M.Jayawardene	143	11319	33	46
S. Chanderpaul	153	11219	29	62
Allan Border	156	11174	27	63

Test Records: Most Wickets

Player's Name	Matches	Wickets	5w	6w
Muttiah Muralitharan	133	800	67	22
Shane Warne	145	708	37	10
Anil Kumble	132	619	35	8
Glenn McGrath	124	563	29	3
Courtney Walsh	132	519	22	3
Kapil Dev	131	434	23	2
Richard Hadlee	86	431	36	9
Shaun Pollock	108	421	16	1

Bye-bye Sachin

Career Statistics				
	Tests	ODIs	T20Is	T20
Matches	200	463	1	96
Runs	15921	18426	10	2797
Average	53.78	44.83	10.00	32.90
Best	248*	200*	10	100
100s	51	49	0	1
50s	67	96	0	16
Bowling Averages				
Balls	4228	8054	15	93
5w	0	2	0	0

Chapter Fourteen

Glossary of Cricket Terms

FIRST-CLASS CRICKET

Cricket is a team sport played between two teams of eleven. It is known for its rich terminology. Some terms are often thought to be arcane and humorous by those not familiar with the game. This is a general glossary of the terminology used in the sport of cricket.

A

All out—when an innings is ended due to ten of the eleven batsmen on the batting side being either dismissed or unable to bat because of injury or illness.

All-rounder—a player adept at both batting and bowling. In the modern era, this term can also refer to a wicket-keeper adept at batting.

Appeal—the act of a bowler or fielder shouting at the umpire to ask if his last ball took the batsman's wicket. Usually phrased in the form of howzat (how-is-that?).

B

Back spin—(also under-spin) a delivery which has a rotation backwards so that after pitching it immediately slows down, or bounces lower and skids on to the batsman.

Bail—one of the two small pieces of wood that lie on top of the stumps to form the wicket.

Ball—the round object which the batsman attempts to strike with the bat.

Bat—the wooden implement with which the batsman attempts to strike the ball.

Bouncer—a fast short pitched delivery that rises up near the batsman's head.

Boundary—1. the perimeter of the ground; 2. four runs. Also used to mention a four and a six collectively; 3. the rope that demarcates the perimeter of the ground.

Bowled—a mode of a batsman's dismissal. Occurs when a delivery hits the stumps and removes the bails.

Bowling—the act of delivering the cricket ball to the batsman.

Brace—two wickets taken off two consecutive deliveries.

Bumper—old-fashioned name for a bouncer.

Bye—extras scored in the same way as normal runs when the ball does not make contact with any part of the batsman (bat, protective gear, body parts).

C

Catch—to dismiss a batsman by a fielder catching the ball after the batsman has hit it with his bat but before it hits the ground.

Caught behind—refers to a catch by the wicket-keeper.

Century—an individual score of at least 100 runs, a significant landmark for a batsman. Sometimes used ironically to describe a bowler conceding over 100 runs in an innings.

Clean bowled—bowled, without the ball first hitting the bat or pad.

Covers—1. a fielding position between point and mid-off.
2. the equipment used to protect

the pitch from rain.

Crease—one of several lines on the pitch near the stumps (the "popping crease", the "return crease" and the "bowling crease") most often referring to the popping crease.

Cricketer—a person who plays cricket.

Cut—a shot played square on the off side to a short-pitched delivery wide of off stump. So called because the batsman makes a "cutting" motion as he plays the shot.

D

Delivery—the act of bowling the ball.

Double—normally the scoring of a 1000 runs and the taking of 100 wickets in the same season.

Double Hat-trick—Taking four wickets in four consecutive balls.

Draw—1. a result in timed matches where the team batting last are not all out, but fail to exceed their opponent's total. Not to be confused with a tie, in which the side batting last is all out or run out of overs with the scores level.

2. an antiquated stroke that has fallen into disuse, it was originally a deliberate shot that resembled the Chinese cut – the ball being played between one's own legs.

Drive—a powerful shot generally hit along the ground or sometimes in the air in a direction between cover point on the off side and mid-wicket on the leg side, or in an arc between roughly thirty degrees each side of the direction along the pitch.

Duck—a batsman's score of nought (zero) dismissed, as in "he was out for a duck." It can refer to a score of nought not out during an innings, as in "she hasn't got off her duck yet", but never refers to a completed innings score of nought not out. Originally called a "duck's egg" because of the "0" shape in the scorebook.

E

Eleven—another name for one cricket team, which is made of eleven players.

End—An area of the ground directly behind one of the stumps, used to designate what end a bowler is bowling from (e.g. the Pavilion End). The bowlers take turns delivering alternating overs from the two ends of the pitch.

F

Fast bowling (also pace bowling)—a style of bowling in which the ball is delivered at high speeds, typically over 90 mph (145 km/h). Fast bowlers also use swing.

Fielder (also, more traditionally, fieldsman)—a player on the fielding side who is neither the bowler nor the wicket-keeper, in particular one who has just fielded the ball. The word fieldsman was ubiquitous until the 1980s, when political correctness compelled the adoption of a gender neutral term.

Fired—to be given out (often LBW) by an umpire wrongly.

First change—a bowler who takes over from one of the opening bowlers.

First-class cricket—the senior form of the game; usually county, state or international. First-class matches consist of two innings per side and are usually played over three or more days.

Follow on—the team batting second continuing for their second innings, having fallen short of the "follow on target". The definition of this target has changed over time, but is currently 200 runs behind the first teams score in a 5 day game, 150 runs in a 3 or 4 day game, 100 runs in a 2 day event and 75 in a single day.

Full toss (also full bunger)—a delivery that reaches the batsman on the full, i.e. without bouncing. Usually considered a bad delivery to bowl as the batsman has a lot of time to see the ball and play an attacking shot. Also, it does not have a chance to change direction off the ground, making it the ultimate crime for a spin or seam bowler.

G

Glove—part of a batsman's kit worn to protect the hands from accidental injury. When a hand is in contact with the bat it is considered part of the bat and so a player can be given out caught to a ball that came off the glove hence "gloved a catch."

Googly—a deceptive spinning delivery by a leg spin bowler, also known (particularly in Australia) as the wrong 'un. For a right-hander bowler and a right-handed batsman, a googly will turn from the off side to the leg side.

Gully—a close fielder near the slip fielders, at an angle to a line between the two sets of stumps of about 100 to 140 degrees.

H

Hack—a batsman of generally low skill with an excessively aggressive approach to batting, commonly with a preference towards lofted cross bat shots. A poor defensive stance and lack of defensive strokes are also features of a hack. Can also be used to describe one particular stroke.

Half Century—an individual score of over 50 runs, but not over 100 (century). Reasonably significant landmark for a batsman and more so for the lower order and the tail-enders.

Hat-trick—a bowler taking a wicket off each of three consecutive deliveries that he bowls in a single match (whether in the same over or split up in two consecutive overs, or two overs in two different spells, or even spread across two innings of a test match or first-class cricketgame).

Hit wicket—a batsman getting out by dislodging the bails of the wicket behind him either with his bat or body as he tries to play the ball or set off for a run.

Hook—a shot, similar to a pull, but played so that the ball is struck when it is above the batsman's shoulder.

"**How's that?**" (or "Howzat?")—the cry of a fielding team when appealing, notable because an umpire is not permitted to give the batsman 'out' unless the question is asked.

I

Innings—one player's or one team's turn to bat (or bowl). Unlike in baseball, and perhaps somewhat confusingly, in cricket the term "innings" is both singular and plural.

K

Keeper (or 'Keeper)—short form of Wicket-keeper.

Knock—a batsman's innings. A batsman who makes a high score in an innings can be said to have had a "good knock".

L

Leg before wicket (LBW)—a way of dismissing the batsman. In brief, the batsman is out if, in the opinion of the umpire, the ball hits any part of the batsman's body (usually the leg) before hitting the bat and would have gone on to hit the stumps.

Leg break—a leg spin delivery which, for a right-hander bowler and a right-handed batsman, will turn from the leg side to the off side (usually away from the batsman).

Leg bye—extras taken after a delivery hits any part of the body of the batsman other than the bat or the gloved hand that holds the bat. If the batsman makes no attempt to play the ball with the bat, leg byes may not be scored.

Leg slip—a fielding position equivalent to a slip, but on the leg side.

Leg spin—a form of bowling in which the bowler imparts spin on the ball by turning the wrist as the ball is delivered, and for that reason also known as "wrist spin". The stock delivery for a leg spinner is a leg break; other leg spin deliveries include the googly, the top spinner, and the flipper. The term leg spinner is usually reserved for right handed bowlers who bowl in this manner. Left handers who bowl with wrist spin are known as unorthodox spinners. This is also known as the Chinaman.

Life—a noun that refers to a batsman being reprieved because of a mistake by the fielding team, through dropping a catch, missing a run-out chance or the wicket-keeper missing a stumping.

Light—short for "bad light." Umpires offer the batsmen the option to cease play if conditions become too dark to be safe for batting.

M

Maiden over—an over in which no runs are scored off the bat, and no wides or no balls are bowled. Considered a good performance for a bowler, maiden overs are tracked as part of a bowling analysis.

Man of the match—an award which may be given to the highest scoring batsman, leading wicket taker or best overall performer in a match. Man of the series is the same over a whole series.

Match fixing—bribing players of one of the teams to deliberately play poorly, with the intention of cashing in on bets on the result of the game.

Medium-pace—a bowler who bowls slower than a pace bowler, but faster than a spin bowler. Speed is important to the medium-pacer, but they try and defeat the batsman with the movement of the ball, rather than the pace at which it is bowled. Medium-pacers either bowl cutters or rely on the ball to swing in the air. They usually bowl at about 55–70 mph (90–110 km/h).

N

Nets—a pitch surrounded on three sides by netting, used by for practice by batsman andbowler.

Nightwatchman (in a first-class game)—a lower order batsman sent in when the light is dimming to play out the remaining overs of the day in order to protect more valuable batsmen for the next days play.

No ball—an illegal delivery, usually because of the bowler overstepping the popping crease, scoring an extra for the batting side. Full tosses that pass above the waist of the batsman are also deemed no balls.

Non-striker—the batsman standing at the bowling end.

Not out—1. a batsman who is in and has been not yet been dismissed, particularly when play has ceased.

2. the call of the umpire when turning down an appeal for a wicket.

O

One Day International (ODI)—a match between two national sides limited to 50 overs per innings, played over at most one day.

Off spin—a form of bowling in which the bowler imparts spin on the ball with the fingers as the ball is delivered, and for that reason also known as "finger spin". The usual stock delivery for an off spinner is an off break, but other off spin deliveries includes the arm ball and the doosra. The term off spinner is usually reserved for right handed bowlers who bowl in this manner. Left handers are described as orthodox or unorthodox.

One-day cricket—an abbreviated form of the game, with just one innings per team, usually with a limited number of overs and played over one day.

One down—a batsman who bats at #3, a crucial position in the team's batting innings.

One short—the term used when a batsman fails to make contact with the ground beyond the popping crease, and turns back for an additional run.

Opener—1. a batsman skilled at batting at the beginning of an innings, when the ball is new.

2. one of the bowlers who open the innings, usually the fastest bowlers in the side.

Out—1. the state of a batsman who has been dismissed.
2. the word sometimes spoken while raising the index finger by the umpire when answering an appeal for a wicket in the affirmative.

Outswing—a delivery that curves away from the batsman.

Over—the delivery of six consecutive legal balls by one bowler.

Over rate—the number of overs bowled per hour.

Over the wicket—a right-handed bowler bowling to the left of the stumps, and vice-versa for a left-handed bowler.

P

Pace bowling (also fast bowling)—a style of bowling in which the ball is delivered at high speeds, typically over 90 mph (145 km/h). Pace bowlers also use swing.

Pads—protective equipment for batsmen and wicket-keepers, covering the legs.

Pavilion—Term for the grandstand or building complex where the player's dressing rooms and members of the association or club owning the ground are seated. The dressing rooms are generally located in the members' area.

Pitch—1. the rectangular surface in the centre of the field where most of the action takes place, usually made of earth or clay. It is 22 yards in length.
2. of the ball, to bounce before reaching the batsman after delivery. the spot where the ball pitches

R

Run out—dismissal by a member of the fielding side breaking the wicket while the batsman is outside his/her crease in the process of making a run.

Run rate—the average number of runs scored per over.

Runner—a player of the batting side assisting an injured batsman in running between the wickets. The runner must wear and carry the same equipment and both the injured batsman and the runner can be run out, the injured batsman having to stay in his ground.

S

Shot—the act of the batsman hitting the ball with his bat.

Silly—a modifier to the names of some fielding positions to denote that they are unusually close to the batsman, most often silly mid-off, silly mid-on, silly midwicket and silly point.

Single—a run scored by the batsmen physically running once only between the wickets.

Sitter—an easy catch (or occasionally a stumping) that should generally be taken.

Six (or Sixer)—a shot which passes over or touches the boundary without having bounced or rolled, so called because it scores six runs to the batting side.

Slip—a close fielder behind the batsman, next to the wicket-keeper on the off-side. There can be as many as four slips for a faster bowler. Also ("in the slips", "at first slip") the positions occupied by such fielders.

Spin bowling—a style of bowling in which a spin bowler ("spinner") attempts to deceive the batsman by imparting spin on the ball using either their fingers or their wrist. Spin bowling is most effective when the ball is travelling relatively slowly, and so most spinners bowl at a pace between 40 and 55 mph.

Square-cut—A Cut shot, played square, i.e. perpendicular to the bowler's delivery.

Strike—the position as batsman, as opposed to non striker. Often, 'Keep [the] strike', to arrange runs on the last ball of an over so as to face the first ball of the next. 'Shepherd the Strike': to keep doing this to protect a less skillful batsman.

Stroke—an attempt by the batsman to play at a delivery.

Stump—1. one of the three vertical posts making up the wicket ("off stump", "middle stump" and "leg stump");

2. a way of dismissing a batsman; or

3. ("stumps") the end of a day's play.

Sweep—a shot played to a good length slow delivery. The batsman gets down on one knee and "sweeps" the ball to the leg side.

Swing—a bowling style usually employed by fast and medium-pace bowlers. The fielding side will polish the ball on one side of the seam only; as the innings continues, the ball will become worn on one side, but shiny on the other. When the ball is bowled with the seam upright, the air will travel faster over the shiny side than the worn side. This makes the ball swing (curve) in the air. Conventional swing would mean that the ball curves in the air away from the shiny side.

T

Target—The score that the team batting second has to score to beat their opponents. This is one run more than what the team batting first managed.

Test match—a cricket match with play spread over five days with unlimited overs played between two senior international teams. Considered the highest level of the game.

Third umpire—an off-field umpire, equipped with a television monitor, whose assistance the two on-field umpires can seek when in doubt.

Throwing—of a bowler, an illegal bowling action in which the arm is straightened during the delivery.

Tie—the (very rare) result in which the two teams' scores are equal and the team batting last is all out (or, in a limited overs match, the allotted overs have been played) . Not to be confused with a draw, in which the scores are not equal.

Twelfth man—Traditionally, the first substitute player who fields when a member of the fielding side is injured. In Test matches, twelve players are named to a team prior to the match, with the final reduction to eleven occurring immediately prior to play commencing on the first day. This gives the captain some flexibility in team selection, dependent on the conditions (e.g. a spin bowler may be named to the team, but omitted if the captain feels that the pitch is not suitable for spin bowling).

Twenty-20—a new, fast paced, form of cricket limited to twenty overs per innings, plus some other rules changes, specifically designed to broaden the appeal of the game.

U

Umpire—one of the two (or three) enforcers of the rules and adjudicators of play.

Under-spin (also back-spin)—backward rotation on the ball, causing it to decrease speed immediately after pitching.

W

Wicket—1. a set of stumps and bails;

2. the pitch; or

3. the dismissal of a batsman.

Wicket-keeper—the player on the fielding side who stands immediately behind the batting end wicket. A specialist position, used throughout the game.

Wide—a delivery that passes illegally wide of the wicket, scoring an extra for the batting side. A wide does not count as one of the six valid deliveries that must be made in each over–an extra ball must be bowled for each wide.